Old School Love

Old School Love

AND WHY IT WORKS

Joseph "Rev Run" and Justine Simmons

WITH AMY FERRIS

DEY ST.

An Imprint of WILLIAM MORROW

DEY ST.

All photographs are courtesy of the authors unless otherwise marked.

HarperCollins books may be purchased for educational, business, or sales promotional use. For information, please email the Special Markets Department at SPsales@harpercollins.com.

FIRST EDITION

Designed by Michelle Crowe
Background Texture by YamabikaY/Shutterstock, Inc.

Library of Congress Cataloging-in-Publication Data has been applied for.

ISBN 978-0-06-293972-2

20 21 22 23 24   LSC   10 9 8 7 6 5 4 3 2 1

We dedicate this book to Justine's mom, Susan Young,
who recently passed, for her everlasting love and support
for the two of us and for teaching us so much about life.

Contents

INTRODUCTION   1

PROLOGUE   6

PROTECTIVE LOVE   13

TOUGH LOVE   21

MAGICAL LOVE   27

TRUSTING LOVE   33

SUCCESSFUL LOVE   41

GOOD LOVE   57

ENDURING LOVE   65

FAITHFUL LOVE   81

UNCONDITIONAL LOVE   91

CONTENTS

GENEROUS LOVE   103

MESSY LOVE   111

GROWN-UP LOVE   125

OUR BLENDED FAMILY   131

ATTENTIVE LOVE   143

POWERFUL LOVE   151

ROMANTIC LOVE   157

OLD SCHOOL LOVE: Part One   171

OLD SCHOOL LOVE: Part Two   185

EPILOGUE   196

AFTERWORD: JUSTINE'S MOM   203

ACKNOWLEDGMENTS   211

ABOUT THE AUTHORS   213

Old School Love

INTRODUCTION

THIS IS A BOOK ABOUT LOVE.

GOOD LOVE. KIND LOVE. RESPECTFUL LOVE. MESSY LOVE. GENUINE LOVE. POWERFUL LOVE. ENDURING LOVE. GENEROUS LOVE. TRUSTING LOVE. COMMUNICATING LOVE. SELFLESS LOVE. ROMANTIC LOVE. TOUGH LOVE.

FAITHFUL LOVE. LASTING LOVE. PROTECTIVE LOVE. GROWN-UP LOVE.

MAGICAL LOVE.

OLD SCHOOL LOVE.

IN 1994 WE SAID: *I do.*

In 2018 we said: *Let's do it.*

WE HAD AN IDEA for a book—one we hoped would inspire and move folks. It's the story of what we have created together through all these years of marriage—our family, our careers, our legacy.

Everything we've built is made up of love—specifically, *Old School Love*.

Yes, our love story is a fairy tale.

We've been married since 1994, a quarter of a century. We have seen it all, heard it all, and now we want to share it all.

Too many couples can barely make it through a year; some last only a month. Many don't view marriage as a lifetime commitment—instead of seeing it as a vow to a lifetime of mutual growth, love, and support, they see it as something to do for now. Something to do on a whim, or between tweets.

We have noticed that many couples throw in the towel when things get a bit rough, when life throws them a few curveballs, when their vows become too much of a burden— too much of a burden to carry out or carry through.

We fell head-over-heels for each other a long time ago, when we were just kids, and then life happened—and then it conspired to bring us back together. Since then, we've learned so much about carrying someone else. We have gone through so much together—grand times, amazing times, and times that have tested our faith and our hearts.

It's in the toughest moments that you need to remember to *live* your vows, and remember why you took them. Believe us, those times show up—like the death of our beloved baby girl, Victoria Ann, and the recent passing of Justine's dear mom, who was battling cancer but died unexpectedly from pneumonia.

What you need to know from the outset is that we're two imperfect people. We bicker and we disagree; we're both strong-willed and strong-minded; we're opinionated and passionate about our needs and desires, but our love is stronger and more beautiful for the wear.

We try our best to be nonjudgmental, to forgive each other; to say I'm sorry as often as needed—and saying I love you is needed often. We know from experience that harsh words are sometimes said in a heated moment, and we have learned through trial and tribulation that words have consequences but that an action taken out of love leaves a lasting impression.

There is a saying that goes something like this: *The greater the obstacle the greater the joy.* Patience is a virtue. You can't have a gorgeous garden or gorgeous flowers without getting down in the dirt; and marriage, well, that's the dirt; it's where you get to plant and sow, weed and prune; it's the witnessing of a seed blossoming.

MARRIAGE IS WORK. Some days it's filled to the brim with joy and laughter and lots of good food, and *some days . . .* some days it's hard work, it's *woe is me* work, it's *can we really do this another day, another week?* work.

But nobody ever said that marriage was easy. Nobody. And chances are if they did, they are no longer married.

They're sitting in some bar or a coffee shop or a diner bemoaning the end of a relationship that more than likely had many, many opportunities for improvement. That's because they forgot to read the fine print in the marriage manual.

It is in the fine print that it says: *Marriage takes work, but it is so worth it.*

There's no way around doing the work, and the work is what brings you closer together. The work is what teaches you about compromising, about forgiveness, about speaking up, about letting go of what no longer serves you, about compassion and generosity and good love, strong love, successful love. The work is what teaches you how to love better, how to be kinder, how to stop needing to be the center of attention and start paying attention to what and who is right in front of you.

Doing the work is what keeps the proverbial flame alive and burning bright, even if it seems to be only a flicker.

This book is a tool for folks—for you, the readers—to get to where we're at after all these years together. This book is to help you shorten that distance, and to share the lessons we wish we'd known sooner. We figure we have some wisdom to impart, some experiences to share, and some stories that you will relate to.

We believe we have the tools and the knowledge and the deep passion to inspire you, to encourage you, to instill some hope about this crazy thing called love. All different kinds of love, and the wisdom we've learned from each one.

Our greatest hope is that you will read through this book

and find a chapter, or a paragraph, or even a sentence, that will stick to your ribs; something that will make you think a little bit differently about what you're doing or saying, so you'll possibly react a little less emotionally during a disagreement, find some beauty in the midst of an argument, see the tremendous value of creating projects together, understand the importance of compassion and kindness and generosity when you're dealing with your children.

This book has been an extraordinary collaborative effort, a grand effort, and we are so grateful to have the opportunity to share our stories and our lives with you so you can become one with the words.

Marriage isn't perfect, but it is perfectly wonderful, and Old School Love is the most wonderful thing of all.

—Rev Run & Justine Simmons

PROLOGUE

Rev

"For every house is built by someone,
but God is the builder of everything."

HEBREWS 3:4

I WAS FOURTEEN YEARS OLD, and fifteen minutes from my house in Hollis, Queens, was a neighborhood called Jamaica Estates.

It was the kind of place that a teenager living in a working-class home could only dream about.

I thought everything about that place was perfect: how some of the houses sat on hills, and some of the houses had white pillars that made them even more intimidating. Some of the houses had gates, and some of them had the kind of landscaping that made you just stand in awe at the beauty.

I liked walking in this neighborhood, and in particular I liked to walk past this home that sat on a hill overlooking the Grand Central Parkway. It had boxwood shrubs lined all the way up the entrance stairs, and the yard was full of flowers bursting with color.

The legend goes that the owner of the house had flowers planted in honor of his wife, ones that would always be in bloom on Mother's Day. I don't know if that story is true, but I like the love behind it, I like the sentiment.

I remember one day I was walking past the house, I thought to myself that this was as good a time as any to talk to God, to ask for a sign. Because you know kids at fourteen, fifteen, we need signs, we need answers, we need something to tell us if we're going in the right direction.

So I stopped and I said aloud, "If a leaf falls right now, it's God's sign that I'm going to get this house one day."

At that very moment—that *very* moment—a leaf fell from a tree.

I wrote a letter, and that letter said: *Dear Sir, I love your home, I will buy this house one day.*

I hurried up the stairs, rang the bell, and I handed the note to the man who answered the door; maybe it was the owner of the house, maybe it was someone who worked for him. And being fourteen, well, that was more than enough courage to muster for one day.

SO, I WENT ABOUT MY BUSINESS, and I more or less forgot about this big act of bravery. And at the time, my business was making music.

Kurtis Blow took me under his wing, and I became known as "the Son of Kurtis Blow." I was his protégé. Kurtis was known as "the King of Rap" and was the first rapper to sign a record deal, setting the stage for the emergence into the mainstream of both rap and hip-hop. In 1979 he released "Christmas Rappin'," which became a big success, and then in 1980, "The Breaks" became the first single to go gold for hip-hop. Whenever I think about Kurtis, I always think of how amazing it is that he was "the King of Rap" and RUN DMC would later be known as "the Kings of Rap." Life is funny that way.

By the time I turned fifteen, I was learning to scratch and I would DJ for him on occasion when he did shows in Queens and on Long Island. That's when I became DJ Run.

One night we were doing a show on Long Island at a roller rink. The young kids got to stand up front for the first show and the older kids had to stand in the back, but after that performance we went to the private club in the back of the space to do another show for older kids, so they could dance and have a night out.

I saw a bunch of girls around my age in the front row. One of the girls wanted to meet me, so after the first show she knocked on the door that led to the club and asked the doorman if she could speak with the guy who was with Kurtis Blow.

That was the night I met Justine. That was the first night I felt *it*. You know, when your heart stops and it feels like it's making its way up to your head and everything goes all fuzzy.

Three girls were standing at the door. I gave the first girl my autograph and a kiss, and I gave the second girl an autograph and a kiss, and then I went to kiss Justine—she was a vision dressed in different shades of blue—and she kissed me back. But then I was whisked away.

Later that night, she handed her phone number to the concessions lady and told her, "Please give this to the guy who is with Kurtis Blow, not Kurtis Blow."

I called her the next day, and I left a message with her stepmom: "Tell her Joe called"—because back then I was Joe, or Joey—and I gave my phone number. Justine called me back, and we spoke on the phone for what felt like months; we wrote letters to each other with little handmade hearts and colored-pencil birds. In one letter that I wrote her I closed with these words: *I will marry you one day.*

After all of the talking and the longing, we set up a double date. The four of us went to the movies, and we had a great time. But I was still living in Hollis, Queens, and Justine was living out in Hempstead, Long Island, and we might as well have been living with an ocean between us.

Time is either on your side or it slips away, and to be honest, it felt like distance made our hearts grow apart, not fonder.

I became a huge rap star at eighteen. My career exploded, and as you can imagine, my life did, too. I didn't see Justine for years after that.

I moseyed on about my life, and pieces of my life were breaking. But on the days when I was Joey, when I wasn't on a stage or recording or being RUN . . . I wondered about Justine.

A few years later, when RUN DMC had become wildly successful, my cousin was working as a security guard on Long Island. One day he was bragging on and on about me. Telling everyone that his cousin was RUN from RUN DMC, spreading it all around. Justine's sister overheard him and said to my cousin, "Oh yeah, so what? My sister Justine used to go with RUN from RUN DMC before he was RUN, before he was famous."

My cousin came home and asked me if I remembered a girl named Justine. Of course I did. I asked him to get Justine's number, and I called her, and I've been calling her, and loving her, every day since.

She kept the letter I had written her: *I will marry you one day.*

The house in Jamaica Estates went up for sale after the owner passed on, but before he died he told his children to find me, to let me know that the house was for sale.

He had kept the letter I had written to him: *Dear Sir, I love your home, I will buy this house one day.*

Both the house and the girl came back to me.

I like to think that life is filled with miracles and

beauty—like the flowers that bloom every Mother's Day. All of the unexpected turns that might seem off track are, in fact, blessings taking me to exactly where I need to go.

My life—my life with Justine—is proof that magic happens.

Protective Love

"A gentle answer turns away wrath, but a harsh
word stirs up anger."

PROVERBS 15:1

Protective love is taking care of the other person, watching out for them. Having their back every single day. Knowing what tripped them in their past relationships, and making sure they feel secure with you. It's paying attention to what they need and seeing the other person—understanding what it takes to secure them up. Learning what you need to do to protect their heart.

Justine

(BEFORE JOEY)

BEFORE JOEY, I wasn't always secure in my relationships—and by "my relationships," I mean with guys.

You know how some people tell you—remind you—that you're insecure, that you're a jealous person?

Some guys do it to make you feel that the problem is you and not them.

"Why are you so insecure?" they'd ask.

"Why are you so jealous?" they'd say.

I believed them when they asked that. I believed what they thought about me.

In truth, though, that was the way they made me feel, and they didn't stop trying to convince me that they were right.

I thought that I needed to toughen up, have a tougher skin. It wasn't until Joey that I realized that people do things that make you mistrust them. They make you believe that you are a suspicious, jealous person, and then you become one, because you start feeling like there's something to be suspicious of.

It took me a while to understand that being around people like that wasn't good for my happiness, my health, or my heart. Being around manipulative people is depleting—it can, and it will, drain the life out of you. People who deplete your joy are bound to make you feel small and insignificant and unworthy. People like that don't want you to be happy; they don't wish you well or cheer you on.

Being around people like that can make you feel less than, not enough.

Before Joey, that's how I felt.

I think a lot of women question their worth or doubt their beauty because someone told them to, or taught them to. Bad partners make women feel that they're not worthy of being loved, not worth the time or the effort.

We all need to find the people in our lives who make us feel beautiful, who make us feel good about ourselves, who support us on the days when we don't feel so good, who make us want to be stronger and braver and more courageous in our own lives.

We all need to find and surround ourselves with people who encourage us, embolden us, lift us, champion us, inspire us—people who love us unconditionally.

When Joey and I finally got together—when we settled down and started getting serious—it was like all that insecurity I carried with me just melted away. Joey never made me feel jealous. He never made me question our love or his intentions. He made me feel completely confident, in me, in us.

Joey makes me feel beautiful; he says very kind and thoughtful things. He'll go out of his way to make sure I feel comfortable and at ease. He looks out for me, makes sure I am taken care of, even though I wasn't looking for someone to take care of me. I was and I am a full-on independent woman.

I was looking for someone to love me—all of me. Someone I could count on to protect me, to make me feel like I'm not alone.

Every morning, before he leaves the house, he kisses me goodbye and tells me he loves me. He'll surprise me with a gift, something I mentioned in passing, because he'll remember that I admired it. He'll get me tickets for a concert or an event that he knows I want to go to. He'll take me to my favorite restaurant—not his, but mine—because I love it.

You know how people have bad days? I have bad nights. I can't fall asleep, and I worry about all the things I need to take care of the next day or the things I didn't handle today.

Mostly I work through it on my own, but sometimes I'll wake up Joey and start complaining about my weight or a project that I'm working on that I can't seem to bring together. Whatever it is, he'll let me get it out of my system, even if it means he sleeps less, because he knows if he doesn't listen I'll spiral out. He just listens and then talks about it, the positive side of the things.

We'll handle it, he'll say.
We'll make it better, he'll say.
We'll take care of it, he'll say.

WE DON'T ALWAYS SEE EYE TO EYE, we're both so strong-willed and fierce and opinionated, but the thing I love so much about Joey is that he'll never dismiss me, he'll never tune me out, he'll never turn away from me, and he'll never belittle me.

We're always looking in the same direction, and we talk stuff through. We let each other be heard. Being heard is so important in a marriage.

I found out over the years if you go to bed angry, you wake up angry. That anger festers and as it builds up, it can tear people and relationships apart.

I won't let that happen with Joey. I like Joey as much as I love him.

He always has my back.

Joey secures me up.

I believe we're all tested in areas like love until we get it right.

I got it right.

Rev

(WHAT MAKES A MARRIAGE WORK?)

WHAT MAKES A MARRIAGE WORK?

You want to know what makes a marriage last? You want to know how to keep it strong? Successful?

Here it is.

Do. Not. Cheat. On. Your. Partner.

Let me repeat that in capital letters:

DO. NOT. CHEAT. ON. YOUR. PARTNER.

Do not be all lovey-dovey on a Friday night and all *I'm going to be taking you out to your favorite place on Saturday night and I'm going to be treating you like a queen on Sunday night,* and then go out partying and clubbing and drinking and carousing the next minute. If you're being sweet to your girl and then go out that night with the boys, and start picking up women like you're a single man with no responsibility, with no wedding band on your finger, that's a problem. And that problem is going to catch up with you; you can't run from that problem.

Do not demean the love you are being given.

Do not betray another person's heart.

Do not talk one way and walk another way.

You either walk the walk or don't walk down the aisle.

Do not disrespect your vows, the ones you made looking that person in the eye on your wedding day.

If you want to go partying and clubbing and carousing and drinking, here's a better piece of advice: Do. Not. Get. Married.

Just stay single. Go on, do all those things, but only if you're not going to get married.

If that's how you live, marriage isn't going to work for you. If you want to cheat: Stay single, be free.

That's all I have to say about that.

TAKEAWAYS

- Ask yourself: Does this person build up your confidence? Do they make you feel more self-assured? Do you feel better able to stand up for yourself by being with them? If you're saying yes to all of those questions, it's time to remove some of the walls you've put up and let the other person build *with* you. There is no such thing as a perfect person—but some people can be perfect for you.

- Remember to speak your truth. The right person won't make you feel like you have to agree with everything they say out of fear that they'll leave you if you don't. If you speak your truth, you won't feel like you have to hide your feelings or betray your own heart.

- Learn to say no; marriage is not something you try on for size to see if it fits. Temptation is not your friend.

- Be honest and forthright, and always look out for what your partner needs. Remember what you vowed: through sickness and in health, through richer and poorer, till death. Marriage is all in.

Tough Love

"Let love and faithfulness never leave you; bind them around your neck, write them on the tablet of your heart. Then you will win favor and a good name in the sight of God and man."

PROVERBS 3:3–4

One of the toughest things about new love is making sure that you feel like you can be yourself with someone. It's hard not to try and impress someone, hard not to embellish some aspects as well as minimize other parts of yourself you think someone else won't like. Sometimes tough love means pushing back on those impulses and really letting someone see you. Make sure that love and faithfulness are core to who you are—and that you are truly letting the core of you shine out.

Justine

(FIRST DATE)

MY FIRST DATE WITH JOEY, the first date we had after not seeing each other for a really long time, wasn't actually a date out . . . it was more like a *date in.*

I couldn't believe that after all these years we were getting together, that we were actually going to see each other again. I wanted to look beautiful. I had my hair teased, I was wearing red lipstick, I had on a beautiful two-piece skirt and blouse and high heels. I felt sexy.

Joey came to visit me at my mom's house for the first time, and I planned to cook him breakfast. I opened the door and immediately had butterflies fluttering in my stomach—just like when I had first met him, when I first laid eyes on him years earlier at the roller rink.

He was wearing denim jeans, a mock-neck shirt, a leather bomber jacket with a hood, and Adidas shell toes. He looked so cute.

All I wanted to do was take care of him, make him a nice breakfast, cook him some eggs.

I wanted him to like me, just like he liked me when we first met, and I wanted to like him, just like I liked him when we first met. I was hoping that spark we'd had years earlier could be rekindled, but I was worried that maybe, just maybe, it was a fluke, a flash, a moment that had come and gone. I wanted to impress him—I *really* wanted to impress him—and I really wanted to please him, and you know what they say: *The way to a man's heart is through his stomach.*

Well, I took just a little, tiny detour.

I made scrambled eggs with everything—and I mean everything—mixed in.

I threw in a whole bunch of seasoning: pepper, garlic powder, onion powder, salt, and some other stuff. I just wanted the eggs to taste so good.

I put the plate down in front of him and he ate the eggs, every last bit.

A few years later, we were talking about that first date, and he admitted to me that the eggs tasted just like chicken. He didn't want to hurt my feelings, so he didn't say anything. That is so like Joey, not wanting to hurt my feelings.

Trying to remain cool and collected with a side of sassy, I'd asked him, "Well, where do you think eggs come from?" And then of course, I admitted that I'd tossed in all that crazy seasoning just to give the eggs a bit of a kick, hoping to win his heart.

We both agreed that I shouldn't make those scrambled eggs anymore.

I still want to impress him, but not with food.

After breakfast we sat on the couch and talked for a while, mostly small talk, mostly telling each other how great it was to see each other again and how beautiful we each looked, and we got to know each other a teeny bit more—filling in just a few of the many empty pages. We were both a little nervous—in a good way, like nervous-excited. Then it was time for Joey to leave and he kissed me and, honest to God, it was like magic.

I know that people always say that a first kiss is magical, and even though this wasn't really, truly the "first kiss" because he had kissed me years before at the roller rink, back then I was one of three girls; on this morning I was the only girl. This kiss was magical, and unforgettable—filled with fireworks—and yes, he swept me off my feet.

If I close my eyes now, I can still remember it; how I felt and what it tasted like.

It's hard to believe that we're going on twenty-six years.

Even now, years and years later, when we kiss, when we kiss passionately, it still feels like that first time.

TAKEAWAYS

- Stay away from trying too hard.

- First dates are nerve-racking, filled with all sorts of what ifs. What if he doesn't like me? What if we don't have anything in common? What if we have nothing to say to each other? What if things become uncomfortable? What if *I* become uncomfortable? What if I'm really not his type? What if he's really not my type? So try to keep the first date simple, natural, and comfortable.

- First dates don't always go perfectly, or smoothly; there can be some bumps in the road. Listen to your heart, listen to your intuition, maybe something didn't go quite as you expected but the person had really good qualities, great potential, there was that "something" worth exploring, worth having another date. Explore those feelings.

- Be yourself, and remember that being you—being yourself—is more than enough.

Magical Love

"Consider it pure joy, my brothers and sisters, whenever you face trials of many kinds, because you know that the testing of your faith produces perseverance."

JAMES 1:2–3

It's innocence. Childlike innocence. It's believing when the whole world is telling you not to. It's the ability to trust that things will fall into place without your assistance. And maybe most important of all, magical love means trusting those early feelings, saying, this is what my soul needs, and I know it to be true.

Rev

(FIRST DATE)

WHEN JUSTINE AND I CAME together after years of not seeing each other, it was literally like a breath of fresh air.

I felt so free being with her, whenever I went to Long Island. "Renewed" is the word that comes to mind.

Justine made me feel renewed.

I was so enamored of her. And let me tell you, it was easy; she was gorgeous, and she treated me with so much kindness. It was almost as if I was starving for that kind of attention, that kind of goodness, that kind of love. I understand when someone says they're running on empty and then someone comes along and fills you up, fills your heart and fills your soul.

Those days, those early days, were like that.

We went to every single amusement park in the New York area: permanent ones, pop-ups, special-occasion parks for holidays like the Fourth of July—if you can name it, we went there. We also went to every single mall: Roosevelt Field mall, you-name-it mall; everywhere and anywhere we wanted to go, we went.

Back then, like most men I know, I would pay attention to the kind of clothes she liked to wear and I would buy her something that I knew she would love. She would love that I did that. By paying attention to Justine, I took the attention off of me, and that became one of the most important lessons for me both in love and in life: It doesn't always have to be about me. It shouldn't always be about me.

I loved being out with her. Justine is like a magnet: people are drawn to her, they want to be near her. She gives off this amazing energy, this lovely soft power, and people crave that. She's got that spark.

To this day we still go back out there, to Long Beach, just to recapture some memories, some of those beautiful moments when we were first together.

One of the most gorgeous memories I have embedded in my heart is one of Justine singing to me on the beach.

If I close my eyes, I can envision her, I can remember that moment as if it were yesterday.

Imagine Justine singing Sade—my God, the sheer beauty of Justine.

Now, let me just say . . . Sade, Anita Baker . . . those singers . . . I was not at all connected to that kind of music back then, I was into a whole different thing, and Justine turned me on to that.

Slow.

Sexy.

Jazzy.

Justine singing Sade's songs to me on the beach, well, that took my breath away. Her voice, the way she moved, the way she looked at me.

Now, years later, I play those songs all the time, and if I'm lucky—and trust me, I am lucky—Justine will sing one or two of those songs just for me.

Just for me.
Just like on that beach.

TAKEAWAYS

- Spark curiosity early on and keep the magic alive by asking questions.

- Do something that the two of you will remember as being just for the two of you.

- Be thoughtful. Be romantic. Bring flowers. Write her a love letter or poem.

- Take her places that bring her joy, excitement; fill her with unabashed delight.

- Try not to talk too much about yourself, or make the date about you.

- Show you're interested in every little thing.

- Don't be a show-off, be a show-up.

Trusting Love

"Trust in the Lord with all your heart and lean not on your own understanding; in all your ways submit to him, and he will make your paths straight."

PROVERBS 3:5–6

To trust another person unconditionally and fully you must trust your own intentions, your own actions, and your own truth. Putting your trust in someone gives them freedom—you are literally giving them freedom to be themselves. For us, so much of trust comes from following God's teachings—and staying true to our vows. Knowing that the other person respects those vows only makes it sweeter.

Justine

(BEFORE MARRIED LIFE)

JOEY AND I DIDN'T have sex until we got married.

Now, for many couples, keeping their hands off each other until their wedding night would be completely and utterly impossible, but Joey and I, we take our vows with God very seriously.

For many people celibacy is out of the question. I know a lot of people who, on their very first date, jump right into bed with each other. I just want to say that this is not at all about being judgmental or being critical about what's right or what's wrong, or what's good for someone. We know a lot of people who had sex on their first date, or a few weeks after they started dating, and their marriages are still solid and strong.

But for Joey and me it was important that we lived our truth, and kept true to our word.

We moved in together for a few months before our wedding, because we simply couldn't stay apart. Even though we didn't have sex, we could not stay away from each other. I think the only time during the day we were separated was when one of us had to use the bathroom. I know, too much information . . . but it's true.

We were together twenty-four/seven.

And when we went to sleep, we did that in separate rooms.

And yes, it was hard.

It took every bit of willpower for us to stay away from each other sexually. Joey and I were, and still are, so very attracted to each other. We find each other so desirable and so sexy.

One night I couldn't sleep, and I decided to go and watch some television instead of tossing and turning, and I happened upon this preacher on TV. This was back twenty-five years ago, and he, this preacher, said, *If you're living with somebody and you're not married, if you're shacking up and not married, God can't work through that, you're not taking the right path.*

I felt like this preacher on TV wasn't just talking right to me, I was convinced that he was talking *only* to me. I was sure that no one else had even seen this preacher on TV before.

Not taking the right path, that's what he said.

That was all I needed to hear, and I woke Joey up and told him I needed to move out of the house.

He was like, *Now? Right now? What time is it?*

I told him all about the preacher, and how we weren't living the right path, and that I needed to do this before we got married.

So, I moved out of the house the next morning, and I moved in with Joey's mom. At the time she was battling cancer, and she was so happy to have me living with her.

And then Joey and I got married, and you can just imagine: it was really, truly like fireworks.

And it still is.

So, here's my very simple statement about our sex life: Joey and I treat each other like boyfriend and girlfriend. Yes, you read that right: we treat each other like girlfriend and boyfriend.

I know a lot of married couples whose sex life is routine—you know, same old, same old. Kind of like doing the dishes every night, or sitting down and watching the same TV shows after dinner. Routine. A lot of married couples whose sex life is more of an obligation, more of a *have-to* than a *want to*; there is no wonder or excitement.

We treat each other tenderly, with great desire and wonder; we're excited to be with each other.

When we're in bed we laugh and joke, and share our deepest desires and thoughts and wants. When we're making love we're not overly familiar with each other, and what I mean by that, what I genuinely mean by that, is that we take our time with each other. We kiss and we cuddle; we look each other in the eyes.

When we're intimate with each other, it's always like a brand-new experience and I think that's what makes it— what makes us—so loving, so exciting, so beautiful.

Rev

(YOU MAY NOW KISS THE BRIDE . . .)

JUSTINE AND I STAYED CELIBATE until we got married, and let me just say right up front, that is not easy to do.

It is not easy to do when you're madly in love and the woman you are madly in love with is so gorgeous, so sexy, so beautiful, and sweet as sugar.

But we took a vow of celibacy, and we stayed true to that vow.

We kissed.

We kissed *a lot*.

But no sex until after we were married.

That took a lot of strength and willpower, a lot of holding back, and trust me, I am not a man who can hold back that easily.

But we took a vow, and like all vows that we take, we made sure to stay the course.

We were married on June 25, 1994, and went to the Grand Wailea hotel in Maui.

A white stretch limousine picked us up at the airport to take us to the hotel. I took out my Kenny G CD because Kenny G has that thing—you know, *THAT THING.* I blasted that CD and looked over at my bride, the woman of my dreams, the woman who made my heart skip a beat, the woman who made the world better, the world more beautiful, the woman who looked at me and I would melt. In the back of that limo, I couldn't keep my hands off her, and the feeling was quite mutual.

To say we devoured each other on our honeymoon would be an understatement.

Waiting to make love to Justine made it all that much more delicious.

And to add a little more spice to this chapter, let me share one more story.

I like this story.

I'm going to keep this one very short and very sweet and leave a lot to your imagination. And yes, this was after we were married.

We were down at Disney World in Florida, and Mickey Mouse and Donald Duck were walking around doing their Mickey and Donald Disney World thing. There were all the rides, the cotton candy machine, kids screaming and hollering and having the time of their lives. Down a ways from the hotel where we were staying was a beach, a gorgeous beach where you could hear the waves and the water lapping.

I got it in my mind that when nighttime came around, when it was dark, I'd take Justine down to that beach.

Maybe we'll just take a nice walk, I thought.

Maybe we'll get our feet wet.

Maybe we'll kiss and kiss more and ...

And nighttime came, and Justine and I walked down to that beach.

The sky was clear, the waves rushing, and the closer we got to the beach, all the sounds from the amusement park started to fade away.

The kids and the rides; the once-bright lights from the roller coaster and the Ferris wheel and the merry-go-round, which now seemed like little dots, little flashes of light, compared to the stars that were twinkling above us. I kissed my wife, and she kissed me back, and everything and all disappeared into the magic of the night.

TAKEAWAYS

- Rushing into love, into marriage, doesn't make it better or more lasting; it often crashes when you're rushing. Good things come to those who wait. I know, a cliché, but it's so very true.

- Even years in, make sure you're not rushing through *everything*, if you catch my drift. Kisses, long passionate kisses—now, that's sexy.

- Remember to keep dating your partner. Even after the honeymoon, you can make it *feel* like the honeymoon if you keep things romantic and sexy.

- Love will be—and has to be—tested, that's how you know it's true love.

- Trust your partner. If you need something, tell them— and let them help you.

- One great gift to give your partner is a thoughtful thank-you for something they do so well to support you. Whether it's listening to you talk through issues at night, or reassuring you of your worth, make sure to thank them. They'll appreciate it!

Successful Love

"Commit to the Lord whatever you do,
and he will establish your plans."

PROVERBS 16:3

It's not about having things or acquiring things. It's not what you have materially, but what you generously give and put into your relationship, like a savings account for love. Success is not what you have under your roof, but what you have deep in your heart. Sometimes, in the toughest of times, it's hard to remember what matters most to you, and hard to focus on all of the good parts of your life. But when you only focus on yourself, or on the things you want to acquire, you're going to bottom out.

Rev

(WHEN MY TOP WAS MY BOTTOM)

"Life is not easy, let everyone stand."

I WAS IN LOS ANGELES for a RUN DMC tour, and we were headlining at The Forum. We were huge. And no one—no one—had a bigger ego than me.

It was all about Run.

I was the King.

Whatever was in my way, I was going to push it out of my way. Being selfish was easy.

Back then my life was filled with fame, gold and platinum records, millions of fans, long days and crazy nights. But being self-centered caught up with me.

When you're on a stage and you're looking out onto an audience, whether it's in Madison Square Garden or in a smaller, more intimate venue, what you see is a mass of people hanging on to your every word, your every song, your every beat. But the guy who was on the stage was not the man I wanted to be. He was a guy who had everything, but didn't know the first thing about happiness.

This is what I had:

The presidential suite at the best hotel.

A shiny, brand-new Rolls-Royce waiting for me at the hotel.

The best indica weed in the whole city.

I was the King of everything, and on this trip, this tour, I was going to be interviewed by *Rolling Stone*. I was going to be on the cover of the magazine.

I got up to the suite, and let me tell you, this suite was massive—an entire floor of the hotel. You couldn't get better than that. There is only one presidential suite in a hotel, only one, because only one person can get that suite. And that person was me.

The first thing I did once I settled in was call up room service to order breakfast.

The guy on the phone told me that they were no longer serving breakfast, but they could bring me something else: they could bring me lunch, or maybe a snack, or something else to tide me over. But that's not what I wanted: I wanted breakfast, and plenty of it.

I asked the guy on the phone, "Whoa, man, do you know who this is? Do you know who I am? Because, you know, I'm Run—Run of RUN DMC."

The manager got on the phone and asked me if I was really Run and I said, "Hey, man . . . yeah . . . I am Run."

"We'll bring you breakfast."

I ordered French toast and bacon and sausage and eggs and maple syrup and orange juice.

My appetite was as big as my ego.

There was a huge Jacuzzi in the bathroom, and placed all around it were these fancy bath products: soaps and shampoos and conditioners and loofah sponges. I decided this was as good a time as any to make myself a bath.

I lit up a joint, ran the water, and poured all the bubble bath into the tub. I turned on the jets and the bubbles started to multiply, overflow, like some crazy wild weird cartoon. I was just sitting there smoking a joint and feeling like Scarface.

I was soaking and smoking weed and the bubbles were everywhere—*everywhere,* spilling onto the brand-new tiled bathroom floor—and I was just having the time of my life because . . . *I was the King.*

I was Al Pacino in *Scarface.*

And then there was a knock at the door, and I hollered: *WHO IS IT?*

It was room service, with all the food I ordered, so I got out of the tub all covered in bubbles, looking like some kind of bubble monster. I put on a robe, let the room service guy into the suite, and I had him roll the cart into the bathroom. I'm pretty sure he knew I was stoned, and I'm also pretty sure he knew that the bathroom floor was going to need to be mopped up.

I waited for him to leave and then I went about my business.

And my business was being back in the tub with a tray of food.

I was smoking weed and eating the French toast I ordered with maple syrup dripping down my chin—dripping straight into the bath filled with bubbles. I turned on the TV from the tub, and I was in heaven.

This is what heaven is.

This is exactly what heaven must look like—that is what I was thinking.

Indulgent.

Outrageous.

Food galore.

EVERYTHING I WANTED was right there at my disposal. With a snap of a finger, by just picking up a phone, anything I wanted, it was mine.

I am the King of the entire earth—that is what I was thinking.

A couple of minutes went by, and there was another

knock at the door, and I was thinking, *Whoa . . . whoa . . . WHOA . . . who could it be?*

WHOA.

Because now I was a little—okay, a lot—I was a lot stoned from the weed, and I'd also inhaled all the food from room service, and so I was going through a whole scenario in my mind, a whole paranoid scenario: *Could it be the weed guy?*

Because I was having weed delivered to the room, because back then, I smoked the best weed and they were bringing it to the hotel, because, you got it: I was the King.

Could it be . . . the guy from Rolling Stone? Because I was going to be interviewed, I was going to be on the cover, because, yes, they were coming to interview me . . . because, yes, I was the King.

Could it be room service? Because they forgot to bring ketchup and I called them up and asked if they could bring me some ketchup because a king always gets what he asks for, even if it is ketchup.

And once again from the tub, I hollered: *WHO IS IT?*

And again, I got out of the tub, bubbles everywhere, and I put on the robe, and I looked through the peephole, and this is what I saw: standing outside in the hallway, at my door, right in front of the suite, was the weed guy, the *Rolling Stone* guy, and the room service guy.

All three.

WHOA is me.

IT HIT ME.

Hit me real hard.

Hit me so hard it knocked me on the side of my head, and I almost fell over.

And I started to get real emotional, seriously emotional. I could feel myself getting ready to burst into tears.

They were all standing in the hallway, all three, at my door.

I asked them from inside the suite if they could all come back in a while. I told them that I needed to get myself together, that I needed some time.

Could you gimme some time? I asked.

I went into the bedroom and sat down on the edge of the bed and started to weep—I just wept. And it was so intense and so powerful because in that moment—in that presidential suite, with all the food, with the best weed, with a Jacuzzi filled to the brim with bubble bath—I had this realization: *I don't just have things—things have me.*

Those things had me in a headlock.

I was choking from, and choking on, all the *things* I had. All the trappings that came from this talent that God had given me, all the stuff, didn't make me happy, didn't bring me joy, did not fill me up, not one bit.

No, the weed didn't make me happy.

No, the shiny Rolls-Royce parked outside the hotel didn't make me happy.

No, the overeating didn't make me happy.

No, the massive presidential suite with all the goodies didn't make me happy.

No, all the fame, all the attention, all the adoration, didn't make me happy.

IT WAS RIGHT THERE in that hotel room that I knew—I *knew*—I needed God.

I needed to understand that God had given me this talent, and I was wasting it, making a huge mess of my life.

I was chasing *the things*. The trappings.

I started thinking about what made me happy, what made me really happy, and I knew: what made me happy was love. What made me happy was being an innocent young man who loved to rap, an innocent young man who loved to DJ, an innocent young man who loved to scratch, an innocent young man who loved to bring people that *diddy-bop* from my music. That pure, unadulterated happiness that came from my swag, that came from inside me.

That innocent young man had disappeared, and a man with an oversize, relentless ego had replaced him. I wanted to get that young man back. I wanted to reel him back in.

I wanted to bring him back home to me.

But I was messed up. Really, truly messed up.

Getting better, coming back to myself, didn't happen overnight. It happened over a period of time, just like getting messed up had happened gradually, like a record that is played so many times that it loses its groove.

I did the interview with *Rolling Stone* and we played The Forum and I came back home.

IT WAS AFTER THAT DAY that I saw how much I was sabotaging my own life.

You know how people say how they lose their way, how they feel like they don't know whether to turn left or turn right? You know how people talk about those big moments, the ones that shake you to your core, the ones you need to pay attention to because they hit you so hard?

Let me tell you what that looks like. It looks like a tornado; it looks like something that comes in and just flattens and destroys everything in your life. Leaving shards and broken pieces in its wake.

It looks like a boxer getting pummeled in the ring.

It looks like a storm-ravaged town; unrecognizable.

I was so lost.

Those are the moments that you either shake yourself up and out of your stupor, or you just keep on getting more lost, walking around in a daze.

That day, in that hotel, in that tub—that was the beginning of my adulthood. Like most rock stars, RUN DMC were never home; the road was our home, hotels were our home. All the touring had taken a toll on my life. My first marriage was deteriorating. I needed to stop sabotaging my own life.

I tell this to kids all the time who want to know what it

was like being on the top, being the biggest rap group, being RUN: *My top was my bottom.*

My top was my bottom.

I want kids to understand that it's okay to have things, it's good to have things, but to not let things have you, or get you, or be you, because that's when it gets bad, and when you can really screw up your life. My first three kids were young at the time and I wanted to be a great father, a great model to them. When you focus on the things and not the people in your life, that's when your priorities get all out of whack, when you start thinking and believing that no one is bigger or better or more important than you—like me on that day in that presidential suite, soaking in a Jacuzzi filled with bubble bath, smoking weed, and eating myself into oblivion.

That's when you get lost. You get so caught up in the people looking up to you—the people who want to be you—that you lose sight of who you are.

It was time for me to straighten up, time for me to get my priorities in order, and that's when I started watching church shows on TV. I would just flip through all the channels and stop on these church shows, hoping that something would ignite me, fill me with much-needed hope and inspiration.

There were all these preachers on TV back then, preaching this, that, and the other thing. Some of their shows were like watching infomercials, not very inspiring at all, but there was this one church show that truly captivated me, with the Prophet Bernard Jordan. He was right in my backyard, in New York City.

At the end of the show they scrolled all the upcoming sites of his preaching tour. Many were out of town—like Houston and Ohio and Colorado and California—but there was one date that was coming up for New York City. It was that upcoming Tuesday.

I scribbled down the number, called the church, and I asked the woman who answered the phone, "Will the prophet be in on Tuesday like it said on television, will he be in Manhattan?" And I was told yes, he would be in Manhattan.

I was going to be there.

I bought the biggest Bible I could find, a huge, monstrous Bible. One, because I'm pretty competitive, so having the biggest Bible was right up my alley, and two, because I figured this Bible—this huge, massive one—must have all of God in it, in all those pages.

When I got there, I sat in the front row, and I promised myself that I'd let my life change. That I would start the climb back up, back to myself. Because let me tell you, when you have everything you could ever want and I mean *everything you could ever want* and it doesn't make you happy, that's when life changes, if you let it.

I needed to find a way, a place, to honor God. I was searching for a church. A place where I could put the pieces of my life back together, a place where I could be nourished. I was looking for a place where I could step into my manhood without having to shrink away from who I was.

Bishop Bernard Jordan—also known as the Master Prophet—stood up, and he began to preach. He stood in the pulpit with his wife, Pastor Debra Jordan, and they both exuded excellence. They were like royalty—regal and classy—and the church was pure elegance. I could feel the wisdom coming from the pulpit, the deacons, the ushers, the choir.

The whole service was mesmerizing, and at the end of his sermon, Bishop Jordan said, "Life is not easy, let everyone stand."

That day, *those words*, changed my entire life. I had come home. I knew that day that I would be coming back again and again and again.

Life had been so easy.

Easy didn't make me happy.
Now, I wanted happy.

BISHOP BERNARD JORDAN LIVED by the idea that you can have things, but you can't let things have you. He was a man of great integrity, a man who was serious about God. He was organized, thorough, and focused, and I was in awe of him. I wanted to become like him.

I knew he was someone who could teach me how to

be strong, not only strong on a stage, but in life, on life's stage.

At this church I didn't need to take a vow of poverty like other churches demanded, and that was important to me because I didn't want to give away or lose what I had earned, what I had worked so very hard for. I didn't want to stop being Run, I wanted to become a better Run.

I learned how to walk with integrity, I learned about the scriptures and about Jesus. I learned about tithing, to not be sloppy or negligent with the resources I was fortunate enough to have. I learned to use the wisdom I was gaining, and to share that wisdom.

When the collar was put on my neck to become a minister, I became Reverend Run. I put on that collar and kept my hat, so I never had to lose one step, one bit, of my swag.

I felt like Clark Kent—I went into a phone booth as Run and came out as Rev Run, just like he came out as Superman. But underneath the collar—my version of a cape—was the same man, but now he was a stronger man, a more confident man; a man wanting to help and save others. I had found another calling, a different stage where I could use my wisdom, my life, my words—the ones I write and speak, the ones I use to inspire and encourage, to ignite hope.

God stepped in and held me and took my hand, and I refused to let go. There isn't a day that doesn't go by that I don't ask God to help me make my life work, my life with my wife work, to help us.

I learned through finding love again that a heart is durable and mighty, and that is what enabled me to give more, to be more, to be kinder.

Now no matter when life comes at me—no matter how hard it tries to kick my butt—I'm immediately healed when I'm with Justine.

Here is something I recently wrote about what loving Justine does for me:

I'M PRETTY SENTIMENTAL THIS MONTH. NOT SURE WHY. BUT WHAT I KNOW IS THAT I'M GOING TO TRAVEL THE WORLD WITH YOU. AGAIN, BY OURSELVES. YOU ARE THE MOST COMFORTING PERSON I'VE EVER ENCOUNTERED. WHEN I'M SAD OR HURTING, BEING WITH YOU, IT'S LIKE ALL MY HURT HEALS INSTANTLY. I ESCAPE EVERY HARSH BLOW THIS WORLD HAS TO OFFER JUST BEING WITH YOU. THANK YOU, JUSTINE, FOR BEING SO KIND. YOU ARE THE BREATH OF AIR IN MY LUNGS. THANK YOU.

TAKEAWAYS

- Be aware of your blessings, even in the toughest times. A big ego is generally accompanied by a big fall from grace, and you need to know who and what matter most to you.

- Know the difference between arrogance and confidence. Arrogance comes from thinking you have nothing to learn, that you know better. Confidence comes from learning deep, profound lessons, so you become wiser, humbler. Make a list of five things you do well. Now make a list of five people who helped you become great at those things. Be confident in what's working, and make sure you give credit to those who helped you along the way.

- Trust in God when life tightens up and gets harder. Trust in yourself. Trust in your own intuition.

- Believe in yourself. Being able to rebuild a life piece by piece after it falls apart is a miracle in and of itself. It takes amazing willpower, strength, and determination to put a life back together.

- It takes amazing courage to walk away from what makes you unhappy, that which depletes your soul. Find the miracle in that life story. Honor that miracle. Cherish that miracle. You ARE that miracle.

Good Love

"Love does no harm to a neighbor;
therefore love is the fulfillment of the law."

ROMANS 13:10

Good love is made up of appreciation. While it's also looking in the same direction, having the same goals, wanting the same out of life, good love is knowing the value of what you have. It's supporting your partner on every step of their journey, swearing you'll always be there alongside. The thing about good love is that it doesn't happen by itself; you have to work at making it happen. So know the things that are unique to and good in your relationship—and make sure your partner knows how much you see and appreciate them! We love doing this through poetry—just little poems we write for each other to find in the house.

By Justine

(A POEM)

I love that we dream about our future together.

I love always wanting to be with you.

I love every minute of every day with you.

I love that you appreciate me.

I love that you calm me down when I go insane.

I love that you are so accommodating.

I love being excited to see you after a whole day.

I love that you still give me butterflies.

I love that we balance each other.

I love that you are the only one in the world that can make me feel special.

I love that you believe in me.

I love doing nothing with you.

I love being in love with you.

I love that you are my best friend.

I love that you are my other half.

I love that you have changed my world for the better.

I love our first kiss.

I love that you love me.

I love cooking for you.

I love coming home to you.

By Rev, for Justine

(A POEM)

Your smile is what I grind for.

I will protect that smile.

My get up and go is tied to that smile.

My behavior and my decisions are tied to that
   smile.

My commitment to God and our marriage fills me
   with joy.

You are the main course.

My love for you turns down the noise, keeps everything soft.

Everything else is background music.

Rev

(SETTING ASIDE TIME)

HOW DO I SET ASIDE time after an overwhelming day?

Let me count the ways.

The first thing I do is I get my pen and my pad and I begin to write poems, love poems, to my love. My focus goes straight to Justine.

At around six-thirty or seven, when things settle down, I get quiet and I empty my head of all the day's business, all the stuff rattling around, all the stuff that maybe needs to get done, or didn't get finished, or we're waiting on to happen, and . . . I watch her. I watch her in the kitchen, I watch her in the living room, I watch her with the kids, I watch her taking care of business, and I start writing about my love for her.

That instantly takes me out of myself, and brings me back to the center, and the center is my love for her; our love for each other.

Now, the folks who follow me on social media, on Instagram, on Twitter, they all know that I love doing this, that this is my thing—writing love poems or little love Post-its or love notes for Justine. It doesn't have to be her birthday or our anniversary or even a special occasion; it's just my way of refilling my soul, replenishing myself, giving myself joy, the joy of Justine.

When things seem to be going left, Justine is what's going right.

I have written thousands of poems for her; *let me count the ways.*

Here's a little post, a little something, I wrote for Justine on Instagram.

Here's an example of a perfect day for me.

Went out with you and did everything and nothing.

Home Depot for nothing.

Picked up a broom from there for nothing.

Went to exchange a blouse of yours, they didn't have what you wanted, so we exchanged nothing.

Thought we was gonna have this great lunch but we both only ate less then half and after eating the corn chips and guacamole, we brought home our lunch.

Basically ate nothing.

But at the end of the day being with you was everything.

I love you, babe.

We do everything and we do nothing.

We can go out and do nothing.

We can go shopping and buy nothing.

We can sit together and say nothing.

We can go food shopping and eat nothing.

Being with you is everything.

Nothing makes me happier.

NOTHING makes me happier.

TAKEAWAYS

- Show your partner just how much you appreciate them. Like we said, one of our favorite ways to do this is through poetry, but that doesn't work for everyone. You could make their favorite dinner—or hey, you could go wild and hire a string quartet to sing their favorite song.

- Put in the time to be romantic; it pays off over and over again.

- When your partner does something you appreciate, say thank you. Being able to call out the specific things you appreciate about them will make them feel even more seen by you.

- Small and thoughtful things add up; sweet gestures make for sweet good love.

Enduring Love

"Consider it pure joy, my brothers and sisters, whenever you face trials of many kinds, because you know the testing of your faith produces perseverance."

JAMES 1:2–3

Love will always be tested. It's very easy to walk away, to turn your back, to give up when things don't go the way you imagined they would. It takes strength and fortitude to make love work, and to find ways to make it last. Life will always test a relationship to see if it is what you really want. And once it is what you want, you never want to let it go. The good you put out into the universe will come back to you—it's what we believe, and we live by that wisdom.

Rev

(IT COMES BACK)

EVERY SINGLE MORNING, before I even get out of bed, I turn on my cell phone and go straight to one of my favorite blogs and read some words of wisdom—quotes or short posts about faith and the universe. Sometimes I skim through and sometimes I read the entire post. It's where I rev my day up (no pun intended).

I've been doing this for years.

Sometimes the blog features quotes; some are just a couple of words, and some are longer and a bit more intense, a bit more thought-provoking.

I wake up.

I turn on my cell phone.

I read the blog.

This is how I start every single day, every single morning, no matter what.

Not so long ago, I went to bed feeling distraught. I had

a lot of stuff going on and I was bothered by many things, and by "many things" I mean stuff that had gone wrong during the week, business deals that were taking up way too much time and worry. Because things felt sour in my business life—which is one of the most important parts of who I am—I felt like everything in my life was weighing on me. I decided to keep to my routines and push through. The next morning I did my usual thing and opened the blog, and this is what I saw: *Your blessing is close by, just focus on what's at hand. What you see as a problem is small. It can always be worse.*

I STARED DOWN AT MY PHONE, looked at those words, and I burst out crying. Those were my words, my tweet, and it was the first time that my own words of wisdom had come back to help me.

It reaffirmed that God knew what I needed.

He knew I needed those words, and he made it happen.

Just like the house in Jamaica Estates, just like Justine, those words came back to me, to encourage me. I was overcome with emotion. I couldn't believe what I was seeing, but then I knew: I knew that God needed me to see, and to believe, that yes, I am a messenger who helps folks to know and to believe what's important; to believe in the greatness of their own lives.

My blessing was indeed close by.

Justine

(GRATEFUL)

IT'S VERY, VERY SIMPLE: Joey's words—whether they are spoken or written—soothe me, inspire me, lift me, they fill me up.

What I am most grateful for in my relationship with Joey is how much he respects me, how much he respects our marriage, and how much he respects our friendship.

We are the very best of friends, and to me that is one of the most important pieces of our marriage, because I feel like I can tell him anything, share with him everything, and by "everything" I mean the good and the not so good, and he is always there for me.

He offers a shoulder.

He offers a hand.

He offers boundless love and compassion.

Joey respects my opinions, respects my decisions; respects my two or three or four or even ten cents.

Joey doesn't see me as "his wife," he sees me as his partner, his co-conspirator, his other half—or his better half. He sees me as a smart businesswoman, and a force of nature.

The other thing I love, simply adore, about Joey is he is so positive. His words of wisdom inspire people all over the world, and I feel lucky to be inspired by him every single day.

He is truly a positive force.

I am deeply grateful for Joey.

TAKEAWAYS

- Trust that God has your back. Trust that when you need a miracle, when you need some magic, when you need affirmation, when you need to believe . . . he is right there, close by, tapping you on the shoulder, saying, *Hey, I got you.*

- Remember that your life has unbelievable power. Even when you're feeling hopeless, there's someone you know saying how great you are, how influential you've been in their own life.

- Trust your words and use them well. If you're having a bad time, write about it. Why are you unhappy? What do you have the power to change? Sometimes seeing things on paper helps. Then, seemingly out of nowhere, the solution you've been agonizing about finding shows up.

- If you feel like you're crashing down to earth, take a moment to stop and grab hold of the things that matter to you. What makes you a better, happier person? Even though it feels like the worst thing imaginable, that kind of crash is an amazing opportunity to change your life.

- Respect is like a boomerang, it will always come back to you: give it and you'll get it.

Rev

(DEFEAT)

DEFEAT DOESN'T MEAN DEFEATED.

We were so excited. We had just closed a deal with Netflix and were moving to Los Angeles for six months, where we were going to start shooting a scripted television series based on our lives: *All About the Washingtons*.

My character was an iconic hip-hop artist who, after a long career and much stardom, decides to retire and be a stay-at-home dad, and Justine's character was his wife, who decides to pursue her own career.

We had filmed the pilot for our show, and everyone was thrilled; there was a lot of buzz, a lot of heat around it, and word came down that the network wanted to go to series.

Five words every person wants to hear who makes a TV pilot: *you are going to series.*

We were over the moon.

We were given a ten-episode go-ahead on Netflix and

were going to film the series on the iconic ABC lot in L.A. I wanted to live in Malibu because I love being near the water, but everyone nixed that idea: the drive from Malibu to the studio lot would be unbearable at rush hour, so Justine found us a perfect house in L.A. for those six months. It was right near a lake and an easy drive to the studio lot.

We were feeling very blessed.

We had done plenty of reality television, but we had never done a scripted show. It was a challenge but we were up for it. The director wanted no improvisation; he wanted us to stick to the script word for word, so we hired an acting coach who worked with us every single night to go over the next day's script. Challenging, yes, but exciting. The good kind of challenge.

After filming all ten episodes, there was a big party to announce the show, and it was promoted everywhere. We were in all the entertainment magazines, all the entertainment blogs; our faces were on billboards all over Los Angeles and New York and all the other major cities.

We, the Washingtons, were coming to Netflix.

Our fans were supportive, championing us, cheering us on. Our friends and family were all tweeting about the show. We were getting accolades and a lot of attention. But while some of the reviews were good, most were lukewarm at best, and some of the critics hated the show. That was hard. Bad reviews are hard to read and hard to swallow. But people—our fans—loved it, and they were binge-watching it. That's what you can do on Netflix, after all, and people were watching all ten episodes in a row.

And then the big questions came up: Will we be renewed for a second season? Will we be getting ten more episodes? Will we be living in the lovely house by the lake in Los Angeles for another six months?

My mind was going crazy.

I needed to know.

Tell us. Tell us. Tell us.

We were playing the waiting game.

Tell us. Tell us. Tell us.

Would we be renewed?

That's what played over and over and over in my mind. Like a Ping-Pong ball going back and forth. Not knowing is really hard. Waiting is really hard. Trying to sit on your hands to not make those phone calls is really hard.

Even the most confident person, the most self-confident person, can be the most impatient person.

And then the call came: *Sorry, Joey, they're not renewing.*

That was not what we expected and definitely not what we wanted to hear.

So, I put on my armor, which is what I do when I'm hurting or feeling disappointed. I told Justine and she was so very hurt; she had fallen in love with the cast and the crew, who had become like family to her. Then I told Michael, our manager, and he was hurt and disappointed. We'd all enjoyed working together, doing the show; we felt we had something special.

I was embarrassed and I hated feeling that way. So, I kept putting on more coats of armor and tried to act all tough, like, *You can't hurt me if I got this armor on.*

I didn't want to let the cat out of the bag and tell folks we weren't being renewed for a second season. But Netflix announced that the show was not being renewed; it was in all the same entertainment papers and magazines that had previously announced the show, and there was no hiding from that.

I was hurting, humiliated, and disappointed, but I did not want to be defeated.

Defeat doesn't mean defeated.

That's a very important lesson in life. Not an easy one, but an important one. I know so many people—amazing artists, musicians, actors, writers—who have had their work, their art, rejected over and over or criticized horribly. Then someone comes along and loves it, praises it, and it becomes a huge success. Everyone I know has experienced some kind of defeat, but the key is always hoping that one person will come along who loves what you do, and shines a light.

And in my family, we're all about doing. So I confronted the defeat by planning our vacations, filling the days with new ideas and new opportunities, keeping busy and trying to figure out what we could do next; how to make the best use of our lives, our creativity, our time.

There is a Japanese proverb that says, *Fall down seven times, stand up eight.*

So I stood up.

I didn't want to wallow in the disappointment I was feeling. Wallowing is self-pity and I did not want to go there; I'm not good at self-pity.

I mustered my strength and found ways to encourage myself and encourage Justine and encourage others who were involved with the show. I focused on being inspired and being inspirational rather than feeling embarrassed and humiliated.

"Endurance," that's the word. I like that word. It's a word that packs a punch, like "determination." The underlining message is to never give up, no matter what.

We, Justine and I, endure always. Maybe we hesitate at first, maybe for a day or two, but we most certainly endure. She watches out for me, and I watch out for her, and we make sure we're both okay. Endurance is such a glorious thing: you fall, you get up; a door closes, another one opens; an opportunity disappears and another presents itself.

And yes, there is magic in endurance: it's allowing a stumbling block to become a stepping-stone.

Justine

(ALL ABOUT THE WASHINGTONS)

I WAS SO ABSOLUTELY SURE we were going to get another season, I would have bet on it. We were having such a good time. I fell in love with the entire cast; they really did feel like a family to us, and when we didn't get renewed, I felt so sad and disappointed, because I was sure all of us would be together for another season or two. We all wanted that to happen.

I was absolutely crushed when we got the call that we were not getting another season. I didn't expect it, and I know that Joey was sad and disappointed, but he can hide his hurt much, much better than me; I wear my hurt like my heart, on my sleeve. He hides his, keeps it out of view.

Joey goes straight into "doing" mode.

Let's do this, he would say, and let's do that, he would tell me, and let's do a vacation in St. Barts, and let's think of other things to do together, other projects, other shows.

Let's keep doing, he would say.

And at first all I wanted to do was be sad and be disappointed and not do anything, but Joey's good at getting me out of my own misery, getting me out of my head, the bad thoughts that twirl around. He's good at encouraging me and getting me back on my feet, getting *us* back on our feet.

And we pulled through and we pushed through the pain and the embarrassment and the sadness together, like we always do, and before I knew it, there were other hopes and other dreams on the table for us to choose from.

REV'S TAKEAWAYS

- First and most important: Defeat does not mean defeated. In your worst moments, the most embarrassing moments, when you feel hurt and pain, allow yourself to feel those things; that's healthy. But pick yourself up, knowing you will have many more opportunities.

- Second: Don't wallow too long in self-pity. Stay there for a day or two, but don't move in with self-pity and certainly don't live there. Everyone gets rejected, everyone has setbacks, everyone experiences disappointment. Whether it's in business or in your personal day-to-day life, the most important thing is to believe and to know that defeat is only temporary.

- Third: Don't beat yourself up when things don't go as you planned, and don't beat yourself up when criticism is tossed your way. Try to let it roll off your back, and stand back up.

- And last: Opportunities are plentiful—please remember that.

JUSTINE'S TAKEAWAYS

- Do not push away your disappointment or sadness as if the experience you had meant nothing to you; spend time grieving the loss of something you loved.

- The loss of a job, especially one that brought you joy, can make you feel useless, discarded, unimportant, undervalued . . . please, don't let that happen. Remember the joy, remember the good folks you met, remember the good times. Keep recalling those moments.

- Find other things to do to keep yourself busy and occupied and happy. Keep moving. Keep going. Keep pushing through. Pushing through is a godsend.

- Appreciate and honor all that you've accomplished, all the new things you've learned, the leap of faith you took, the challenges you took on. How brave you were to step out of the box.

- And if you're lucky like me and have a great partner—a great spouse or friend—who helps you get through the tough times, the disappointments, the crushing blows, make sure to thank them for having your back and holding your hand and holding you up.

Faithful Love

"Many claim to have unfailing love, but a faithful
person who can find?"

PROVERBS 20:6

*Faithful love is more than being faithful to the person you're
married to. It's recognizing the vows you took, and the commitment
you made, every day after the marriage. We think there's something
so beautiful about recommitting to the same person and renewing
your vows over a lifetime. Committing to a life of watching the
person you love change, watching them succeed, swearing to always
be their biggest fan. More than that, committing to being your own
biggest fan, as well! For us, so much of the joy of marriage comes
from knowing that our path is illuminated by God, and that he is
always watching over us. That he wants the best for us as a couple,
and for us independently.*

Justine

(GOD AND FAITH)

RELATIONSHIPS TAKE TWO PEOPLE renewing their love, their commitment, consistently. Commit to being faithful. Commit to your intention. Commit to walking beside each other, with each other, for each other.

Commitment is all about renewal. It is not something you do once, and then go about your daily life; it is something you do constantly.

Our entire marriage is based on our faith in God.

It is the foundation on which we stand, it is the structure, it is the walls, it is the windows, it is the floors, it is the cabinets, it is the curtains, it is the rugs, it is the furniture; it is every single room in our home. Our house is built from our faith in and love for God.

It is why we stand strong, and stand by each other and with each other and for each other.

I think a lot of people, if they looked at their marriage, at their lives, through God's eyes, they wouldn't do a lot of things that they do. They would live differently.

We are answering to God, because we know he is watching—and watching over—us. Always protecting us, looking out for our best interests. There's no part of me that doubts that God loves us.

That unconditional love is why we live right and why we live honestly. We try to be kind and understanding and comforting to each other, and to our children, our neighbors, our friends. I like to think we'd live this way anyway, but everything we know to be true and good is because of God. He is why we are faithful to our marriage and our values, why we resolve to treat each other with kindness.

Because we focus on God, we do not permit ourselves to cheat or to be selfish or cruel. We care more about each other, take better care of each other, take better care of the world, take better care, period.

Because if you know how God works, you are going to do as God does, you are going to live his words.

Faith in God is our whole marriage.

I always believed in God, always, but I didn't always go to church. But I have never abandoned God, and he has never abandoned me. God lives deep inside of me, in my heart, in my soul—and in the ways I choose to live every day.

I'm so tremendously grateful for the life God has allowed me to have: this extraordinary life with Joey and our kids, with our families and the people with whom we surround ourselves, who we are so fortunate to call our extended family. I take none of it for granted.

I AM AN INDEPENDENT WOMAN.

I have been independent my entire life.

I want my daughters to be independent, to think for themselves, to stand firm in their lives, to stand up for themselves.

I try to show my daughters through example—*my* example, my words and my actions and my deeds—the importance and necessity of being independent.

I also want them to be able to come to me when they have a problem, or need advice or a shoulder to lean on. I want them to know that no matter what, I am here for them and with them, and together we can work through anything.

I know people often confuse my being with Joey all the time with being too dependent on Joey, and that's not true. The two of us are always working together on our TV shows and other projects, but the truth is that we enjoy being together all the time.

What isn't true, what's a misconception, is that he is somehow the boss of me, that what he says goes, that what he says is the final word. Let me just say for the record, that is so far from the truth.

Like off-the-charts far from the truth.

Growing up around the women I was raised by, I watched

them stand tall around the men they were with: their husbands, their business partners, their boyfriends.

That taught me an invaluable lesson: We don't have to stand behind our husbands; we don't have to be in their shadow; we don't have to stand in the background or off to the side. We can stand side by side, we can stand right next to them, we can stand *with* our husbands.

I grew up around a woman, Pastor Debra, who preached the word of God in the pulpit that she shared with her husband.

I grew up around a woman, my nana, who was so strong-willed and determined that she didn't let anything or anyone get in her way.

I grew up around a woman, my stepmom, Daisy, who came into a relationship with a man who had a few children and an ex-wife, and she took on my dad and me, and she was the glue that kept us tight and centered.

I grew up around a woman, my mom, who looked cancer right smack in the eye and said, *I will beat you, I will not let you win, I will fight you tooth and nail,* and she wore her courage and her bravery magnificently.

Joey and I are equals.

We are true equals in this marriage, and by equals I don't mean fifty-fifty.

I mean we each give 100 percent of ourselves: 100 percent to our marriage; 100 percent to each other; 100 percent to our family; 100 percent to the work we do together; 100 percent to God.

I don't have to ask Joey if I can do something. I don't need his permission or his approval, and Joey certainly doesn't need my permission or my approval.

We love being with each other.

We are bound to each other by love, not obligation.

We want to be together, to hang out together, to do things together.

We respect each other, deeply and mightily.

Being respectful of each other is the key to a successful marriage. For me, people often confuse it with being subservient or submissive. With me standing in the shadow of Joey (and we all know that Joey can cast a huge shadow).

Yes, Joey is a force of nature.

But so am I.

YOU WON'T FIND ME HIDING OR COWERING, or not saying what's on my mind or what's in my heart.

What you will find in me, Justine, is someone being reflective, being conscientious, being cautious of what I am saying because we all say words that we wish we could take back. We all say and do things that we wish we could rewind.

So, yes, I try to be thoughtful, to withhold my words rather than withdraw my words. We take pride in knowing each other's likes and dislikes, being aware of pushing each other's buttons, not saying and doing things that we know would be hurtful or harmful to each other.

I try hard to please Joey, and Joey tries hard to please me. And we both try hard to please God.

I ask myself, *Why would I even want to hurt Joey?*

For what reason would I ever want to be mean or cruel?

Why would I do something out of spite?

Why would I cause him to feel uncomfortable or embarrassed?

What would I gain by doing that?

For example, and this is a really small example but a really meaningful one: I'm not going to wear something that Joey thinks is inappropriate, or something that would embarrass him, or make him cringe.

We go to a lot of events, and I love getting dressed up. I love wearing fancy, beautiful gowns. I love wearing sequins and stunning pieces of jewelry. But I'm not going to put something on that will make Joey ask, *Why are you wearing that?* If he doesn't like something I have on, he'll tell me. Just like I'll tell him if I don't like something he's wearing.

And that doesn't mean that I dress for Joey, and it doesn't mean he dresses for me. It means that I'm aware of making him feel uncomfortable. I want him to look at me and think I'm beautiful and sexy and gorgeous, and yes, the woman of his dreams.

I like when I walk down the staircase in our home and he looks up at me with so much love and so much affection and so much appreciation, like I'm the most beautiful woman in the world.

I love when he looks at me and smiles that big gorgeous smile of his. That makes me feel so beautiful.

I love when we're out and about, and he feels so proud being with me.

I love when he looks at me and says, "You look so gorgeous, Justine."

I think what happens a lot of times is that, when you're first dating someone, you're all excited about that person, you're crazy about that person, that person rattles your life and shakes your world and you do things to make that person happy. You do things to make that person fall more and more in love with you; you don't rock the boat because rocking the boat will cause waves, and we all know that waves are bumpy.

Then you get married . . . you say "I do," and then you *stop doing*—you stop doing all those things that made that person fall deeper and deeper in love with you. You stop wanting to please that person; you stop wanting to make that person happy; you stop wanting to look beautiful for that person; you stop being who you were when you were dating, because now you got the person you so desperately wanted.

And then all of a sudden you wake up one day and you wonder where that person went, that person you were dating who was so hot and so sexy and so very pleasing; *that person* was thoughtful and loving and considerate; *that person* wanted to please you.

I see that in a lot of marriages.

I see that in a lot of people.

I see that just walking through a mall, or walking down the street; it's not too hard to tell when people are no longer happy with each other.

What's that saying, *You can drive a truck through the distance that's between them?*

Joey and I try really hard to make each other proud every single day of our lives together.

We are deeply proud of each other, deeply proud of our faith and belief in God and what he, God, means to us. We are deeply proud of our accomplishments and successes, together and separately, and we are deeply proud of how we are in both our own world—within our own family—and out in the world at large. How we handle all the good things and how we handle all the awful things, and how we look to each other, at each other, in good times and bad.

TAKEAWAYS

- Once you put your faith in God, don't question it, and don't question him.

- God is with you always, not just in a church or in a house of worship. God is in your heart. That is where he lives.

- Renew your vows with your partner; recommit to your intention. Ask your partner, "What do you hope for, for me? For us?" Taking the time to recommit to your values and share your wishes for the marriage will only make your relationship stronger.

- Don't forget: You can still be independent and be your very own person. You can share your entire life without losing yourself or giving away any pieces of yourself.

- Sharing your life doesn't mean giving up your own life. Hold on to the activities that make you independently happy. Make sure you spend quality time with friends and family one-on-one. Having those wonderful hobbies and relationships on your own will only serve to sweeten the ones shared with your partner.

Unconditional Love

*"Finally, all of you, have unity of mind, sympathy,
brotherly love, a tender heart, and a humble mind."*

1 PETER 3:8

*Our love is unconditional—we love and support one another no
matter what. We're partners in life, and we're partners in faith.
Unconditional love is bigger than us—it's about our separate
relationships with God, as well as our shared relationship with
God. Unconditional love requires the willingness to always open
your heart a bit more—to see the world differently, to find comfort
in your faith. Unconditional love means being tender and humble.
Selfless and grateful.*

Rev

(MY FAVORITE SCRIPTURES)

I WANT TO SHARE SOMETHING that's very important to me, something that means the entire world to me: my love of scripture.

I want to share why and how scriptures sustain me when I'm feeling distressed, when I'm feeling a bit like my world is crashing in. How they raise me up even higher when I'm feeling joy, surrounded by goodness and all the beauty in the world.

I was asked recently what my favorite scriptures are, and I didn't need to think hard about it. I didn't need to think long about it. I have favorite scriptures that I recite from memory, that I repeat aloud and say to myself in prayer.

Maybe you're like me and you have profound, deep faith. Or maybe you're questioning your faith and need a bit of wisdom, strength, a little nudge. Maybe you're teetering and wondering if there is a God at all; maybe the world feels a bit heavy, overwhelming, and you need to find God and open your heart to him.

Maybe.

Whatever place you're in, I hope this gives you comfort.

My favorite scripture in the Bible is Psalm 34:4: *I sought the Lord, and he heard me, and delivered me from all my fears.*

Some of the pressures that I have felt over the years being Rev Run have caused me stress and discomfort. Truthfully, going from Run to Rev Run was a big challenge and sometimes felt impossible, but I believe that when I sought the Lord, he heard me. That he delivered me from all of my fears.

Look, we all have fears. We all have worries. We all have hardship. We all have doubt.

We all have sleepless nights. We all look for answers.

We all seek out hope. All of us do this. It doesn't matter if you're rich, poor, beautiful, kind—none of that matters. What's important is that many people pray in times of distress, in times of trouble, in times of great worry and great need. They don't know in their heart if God is listening, if God hears them; they don't even know if God exists at all.

They pray out of fear, not hope.

Here is something very important that I discovered a long time ago: when you have nothing left but God, you have all you need.

When people talk about falling to their knees, when they feel abandoned by their own life, when they have nothing left and nowhere to turn, that's when things get real. That's when you can let in some light. That's the moment. When you have nothing left to lose you have everything to gain.

My mind and my heart are both so deep about God. My mind and my heart are steeped in God.

God, who owns many mansions on the hills; God, who has the whole world in the palm of his hand; God, who can deliver you from any situation.

Mark 11:24 says: *When you pray, believe.*

Matthew 7:7 says: *Ask and it shall be given.*

My faith is so deep because I've been in situations that caused me great pain and great suffering. Out of all the scriptures, the one that touches me the most, that cuts deep and goes deep in: *I sought the Lord, and he heard me, and delivered me from all my fears.*

I imagine there are people—many, many people—who pray occasionally but not continuously. People who get down on their knees once in a great while, people who go to church every so often, people who don't develop a relationship with God. And by relationship I mean an everyday kind of thing where you talk to God, where you seek out God, where you have a conversation with God. Yes, a conversation.

Because even though you cannot see him, you can talk with him, you can lay down your deepest fears and greatest worries with him, you can cry like a baby and share your tears and sorrow with him.

I have conversations with God every single day.

I imagine there are many people who just throw a prayer up in the air kind of like they're tossing a Frisbee, hoping that God catches that prayer—hears their suffering, hears their pain.

There is no hope in *hoping God will hear you;* there is no hope in that kind of prayer. That kind of prayer is more like a wish.

Everyone needs hope. It's why we pray.

We are looking for hope.

Jesus often prayed like this; *Father, I know thou hears me.*

Why did Jesus say, *Father, I know thou hears me?* Because he knew that he was being heard. He already knew it.

This is how I pray.

I already know it.

I live like that.

We, Justine and I, live like that.

The key to life in prayer is not guessing or questioning that he, God, hears you.

I want people to pray, to embrace prayer, the same way Jesus did, knowing they will be heard. I want people to believe in the power of their prayer because prayers travel far and wide, reaching all corners and crevices.

The answer to your prayer will come in time, either in the time you want, or it'll come a little later, or it'll come a little after that . . . but the answer to your prayer will always come in time, in God's time. God's time, which is way different, completely different, from real time, my time, or your time, or I-need-it-now time, I-want-it-now time, give-it-to-me-now time.

SO, I SOUGHT THE LORD, *and he heard me, and delivered me from all my fears* is my favorite scripture because when you read the words, when you listen to the words—*I looked for him and he heard me, and he delivered*—it brings hope.

It brings peace of mind.

When I think of people who don't really believe they're talking to God, who don't really believe in their heart they're being heard, I think back to that scripture from the Gospel of Mark that says: *When you pray, believe.*

When you pray . . . believe.

It's so very simple and so very hard.

YOU NEED TO HAVE FAITH. Have faith in yourself, in the world, in your dreams, in your wants and desires, in others. You need to have faith when it seems the most difficult, when everything feels like it's falling apart.

Another scripture talks about asking for wisdom. New King James reads: *If any of you lack wisdom, let him ask of God, that giveth to all men liberally, and upbraideth not; and it shall be given him.*

Ask for wisdom and God is more than happy to give it to you, *but . . . don't even ask for it if you don't believe he's listening.*

Don't even ask. That's some big stuff right there.

Don't even ask if you don't believe.

Because that's just like a tumbleweed spinning and rolling down a dusty road; it just keeps rolling and spinning and rolling—kind of lost, not knowing where it's going.

So, I pray that prayer quite often, too.

Father, I need wisdom for the situation.

God doesn't just want to give me wisdom, he's *excited* to give me wisdom. God can't wait to tell me how to get out of this situation.

But my favorite part is New King James: *But let him ask in faith, with no doubting, for he who doubts is like a wave of the sea driven and tossed by the wind.*

The whole tumbleweed thing, right there: *blown and tossed by the wind.*

It's kind of like: you asked for wisdom, but you didn't believe, so then why are you even asking?

My soul, my heart, my life, is deep into praying at night knowing that I'm heard, and I'm like an excited child, waiting for the answer.

A while ago I realized that there is nothing more extraordinary than an innocent child waiting on Christmas morning to run to that Christmas tree, lit up with lights and draped with tinsel and pretty ornaments and dangling glass balls just the night before, and then rushing toward that tree knowing, KNOWING, that there will be something under that tree with their name on it.

Now, that's what having faith is, that's what belief looks like: an innocent child, an excited child, waiting for the morning to come.

I know that kind of excitement, that kind of innocence. Especially when I pray for a situation in my life and God answers quickly.

THE BIBLE SAYS, *Weeping may endure for a night, but joy comes in the morning.*

Joy comes in the morning.

Pretty much every morning I put something up on Instagram and this is something I wrote one day: *I'm going to help somebody here today.*

I'm going to let you in on a truth: when I post or write or share those words, *I'm going to help somebody here today,* what I'm really saying is *I'm going to help you and I'm going to help myself today,* because by helping someone else, I'm lifting up my own life. By lifting you, I lift me. And when you lift another person you stand taller, you stand straighter.

I'm going to help somebody here today.

Here's God's pattern, with a scripture to back me up, 1 Peter 5:10: *After you have suffered a little while, the God of all grace, who called you to his eternal glory in Christ, will himself restore, confirm, strengthen, and establish you.*

In the same post I wrote: *Don't let the suffering fake you out, wait on the Lord.*

Again, *the God of all grace who called you to his eternal glory in Christ will himself restore, confirm, strengthen, and establish you,* but it also says *after you have suffered a little while*—which means God is into this, he wants you to go through this, for whatever reason.

NO ONE ESCAPES SUFFERING.

No one. It doesn't matter what your identity is—you're not immune to suffering.

We all suffer. Our problems may be different, may look different. Our losses may be different, may look different. Our pain may be different, may look different. Our struggle may be different, may look different.

But with suffering comes compassion.

With suffering comes knowing.

With suffering comes kindness.

With suffering comes goodness.

With suffering comes generosity.

With suffering comes tenderness.

With suffering comes love.

I sought the Lord, and he heard me, and delivered me from all my fears.

I wish that for everyone: to be delivered from all their fears.

Justine

(SELFLESS LOVE)

MY ADVICE TO EVERYONE and anyone is this: please, don't be selfish. You need to think about the other person, what they want, what they need. Being selfish keeps people small, keeps people from engaging with others, keeps people from being fully present and fully aware in a relationship. Being selfish means not caring enough about the other person, and making it all and always about you.

Selfless love looks like this: communication, listening, paying attention, compromising, trusting.

If you're scared to talk about what's in your heart, scared to share your feelings, scared to tell someone what bothers you, what annoys you, what irritates you, scared to tell the truth, than maybe you're not with the right person.

Joey and I talk about everything. We don't always agree about things, we don't always feel the same way; that wouldn't even be natural. Joey and I, we get short-tempered and have disagreements. There are lots of days when we bicker.

Sometimes he doesn't like what I have to say, and sometimes I don't like what he has to say. Many times we make a decision to not talk until we've let off some steam; we take some space, maybe Joey reads from the Bible, maybe we just sit quietly for a few minutes. One of the things that I have learned is that if you act out of emotion, or react emotionally, or get on each other with anger, then that spreads out. That's how grudges begin, that's how wedges get bigger. You need to know what grounds you so the fights don't cause rifts, and so things don't fall apart and fall away.

At the end of the day, when you get into bed, and the person you love is next to you, that's the best feeling in the world. You can fall asleep knowing that they carry your heart in theirs. So Joey and I don't let our anger spread. Joey and I carry each other.

REV AND JUSTINE'S TAKEAWAYS*

I know that not everyone reading this book is a believer, so my advice is simple:

- Trust that there is a purpose to your life—and that you will find a way out of the toughest situations.

- Ask for help. The people in your life want to support you—but they won't be able to if you won't let them.

- Think about the other person: what they want, what they need.

- Let some steam off—take a walk or some time alone, do some exercise or yoga or journal.

- Try not to react in the moment.

- Communicate, communicate, communicate.

- Learning how to compromise is so important in a marriage—not having to be right all the time.

- Believe in goodness and kindness.

- Have faith in the lulls, the stillness in life; trust in the quiet because that's when you can hear; have faith that your prayers will indeed be answered at the right time; be patient, be self-aware, be self-loving, be humble.

Justine

(FIRST TIME PREGNANT)

I COULDN'T WAIT to have a baby with Joey.

Could. Not. Wait.

When I found out that I was pregnant, which seemed to happen almost miraculously, we were so happy, so thrilled, so over-the-moon excited. All my bonus kids—Vanessa, Angela, and JoJo—were thrilled to have another baby to add to the family, another baby in the house.

It seemed that I had gotten pregnant on the very first day, or night, of our honeymoon. There is some speculation whether Diggy was conceived the very first night after our wedding, in our hotel in New York City, or the second night in the hotel in Maui where we started our official honeymoon. Even though it had only been hours of abstinence, by the second night it felt like we hadn't had sex for what seemed like forever—a few years at least—and I just remember all of it being magical and sexy and

Generous Love

"Remember this: Whoever sows sparingly will also reap sparingly, and whoever sows generously will also reap generously."

2 CORINTHIANS 9:6

It is kindness tripled. It is what keeps the magic in your marriage, in your family, in your lives together. Generosity is what allows your blessings to come back to you twofold. It's a heaping of compassion, and an extra side of unconditional love. It's going that extra mile, the extra distance for someone else, allowing another person to shine. Giving is easy when you have plenty; generosity is what makes life plentiful.

amazing and, yes, fireworks and shooting stars and galaxies colliding.

Being married to Joey, the man of my dreams, being in his arms; feeling the unconditional love of a man I had grown to love so much, was more than a dream come true, because I didn't believe I could dare dream this big.

We were married on June 25 and Diggy was born on March 21. Yes, nine months later.

I loved being pregnant. I loved carrying Joey's baby. I loved all the attention he was giving me and all the attention I was getting; I loved all the care that was being showered on me. Being pregnant has a lot of advantages: folks let you get ahead on line, they offer you their seats, they help you in the grocery store. They help you in the mall, they help you in the parking lot, and we all know how people hate giving up their parking spaces; people are especially kind and generous to pregnant women. The one thing I didn't particularly like was all the food cravings I was having and all the food (and money) I was wasting (morning sickness, hello!), but I certainly loved watching my body grow, feeling all the movements of the baby inside of me, the kicking and the pushing, knowing that I was going to give birth to a baby that was truly conceived and born out of extraordinary love. Insatiable love.

Sometimes, even now, I wish I was young enough to get pregnant again, but I know I would never be able to take care of another child. I get why they say having a baby after forty is not the prime age or time, although I do know women who have gotten pregnant after forty—a complete surprise—and are loving every bit of it. I guess for me, it would be too much to be chasing a baby, taking care of a baby; it is such a massive responsibility, one you can't fake, and I like that our kids are grown or growing up.

I love the brood we have.

Rev

(JUSTINE'S FIRST PREGNANCY)

WE WEREN'T HAVING SEX until we got married.

We got married on June 25. The doctor told us if the baby was conceived on the day that we believed he was conceived on, then the baby would be born on March 21.

Nine months later, on March 21, Diggy was born.

That's called a miracle in my book.

We got married, we got pregnant, and we had a baby nine months later.

I was so excited about marrying Justine. This magnificent angel, my angel, was marrying me, and we were going to have a life together, and we were going to have babies—children—together, and I felt like my life was full of goodness and magic and miracles.

Getting married was truly as if we were being renewed. We had gone years without touching each other, without consummating our relationship, our love; we had made a vow, a promise to be celibate, and we kept that vow, and then we were married and it felt as if our lives were made brand-new.

I believe that if we had made love before we were married, the thrill of her getting pregnant still would have been amazing, without a doubt, but this . . . this was excitement quadrupled. There was so much intense magnetic energy between us; we were finally together as husband and wife and our passion for each other multiplied. We were, and are, so very passionate about each other.

To know that our love created another human being (human beings) still to this day fills me with emotion. When Justine got pregnant with Diggy, we both felt so wildly excited because everything, and I mean everything, seemed so mystical and magical, so miraculous. It was as if God wanted our lives to be filled with overflowing, abundant joy.

I pampered her, and there was nothing I couldn't and wouldn't do for her, to make her more comfortable and more comforted. I loved watching her belly grow, knowing that we had made a baby together. Anything she wanted, any indulgence, any food—even though she could barely keep down many foods she craved—I loved providing for her. I loved taking care of and nurturing her.

And then, right on time, like clockwork, on March 21 Diggy was born. Preparing the room, making it an absolutely perfect nursery, and then watching Diggy grow, watching him go from being a baby to a toddler, watching him holding a microphone in his hands at two years old acting like he was rapping—it was an explosion of happiness. Everyone called him the Golden Child.

He was blessed from heaven, and our marriage was blessed from heaven.

How did I feel about being a dad the second time around with Justine? It was bright and sunny and heaven on earth.

BY THE TIME *Run's House,* the reality show about our family (or as I sometimes refer to it, *Father Knows Best* on steroids), hit MTV, we were following Old School principles with our own personal flair: a rapper who became a reverend and his wife and their brood.

The world was watching us as we, a growing family, were going through growing pains. While we were going through the mundane: the kids growing up right on television, playing and hanging out together. And the typical: family disagreements and family meals and family get-togethers. And the very hard and the heartbreaking: the death of our baby girl, Victoria Ann. The show ran for six seasons.

I LOVE ALL MY CHILDREN.

Each one brings me joy and makes me proud to be their dad.

Messy Love

It's junk drawers and dishes in the sink. It's the good, the bad, the
ugly, the crazy; the spill on the carpet, the unmade bed, the expired
milk in the refrigerator. It's everything—life at its best, life at its
saddest, life at its most joyful, life at its hardest, life in all its glory
and in its darkness. It's complicated, and through the darkness
comes beauty. Through these messy, seemingly impossible times, we
remember we are human—and the most we can do is love, believe,
and have faith we'll come out the other side.

Rev

(VICTORIA ANN SIMMONS)

I GOT UP at five every single morning to pray for my baby.

Imagine waking up every morning for months and months at the crack of dawn to pray—to cry out to God—for the health and the *survival* of your baby. There was something wrong with our baby, the baby that Justine was carrying. There was something horribly wrong.

I got down on my knees every single morning, and I asked God to remove this burden—this burden of a disease—with the full belief that he was going to do it. God was going to deliver a healing, and Justine was going to deliver a healthy baby.

My faith was so deep that I believed it was going to happen; our baby would be healed.

After all, I was a man of God, a reverend in the church, Reverend Run, and I believed in miracles.

But let me backtrack to the beginning.

Justine said to me one day, "Joey, I wanna adopt, let's adopt." We had two children already, and it just never entered my mind to adopt a baby. To me it was about *having* a baby, not adopting a baby, and if we were going to have another child, we would make that happen on our own.

Justine went along with me, and we put adoption on the back burner. We stopped using contraceptives, and almost immediately she was pregnant. We were delighted.

We went to the OB-GYN, and all seemed fine and good. Justine started taking vitamins and all the right nutrients during the first trimester, and she started to show, a little baby bump. That's right around when we went back for another OB-GYN appointment and we were told that there was a problem with our baby.

"Profound" was the word the doctor used.

The doctor gave us a few choices.

Abortion was never an option for us. We had such strong faith, an unwavering belief, that our prayers could turn this into a miracle. We had heard stories about birth miracles, and we held on to those stories. They were happy stories.

God was going to make this right.

The months went on, and so did my crack-of-dawn morning prayers.

Justine was getting bigger and eating like there was no tomorrow. I remember there was one day, I tried complimenting her, even though it was a backhanded compliment. "You look really big," I said, and of course she shot me one of those looks that stops you right in your tracks, a look that has absolutely no words attached to it. Yeah, *that* look. So, I backtracked: "You know, baby-big, you look really nice." But she was having none of it.

I promised Justine that whatever she wanted to eat, I would fulfill that request.

"Hooters, Joey, I want the wings."

I was a man of God.

I wasn't going into Hooters.

No way.

"You promised, Joey, remember you promised? I want wings."

This was a tough call.

I didn't want to go to Hooters, but Justine craved those Hooters chicken wings.

"You made a promise, Joey, you never break your promise, Joey."

So what did we do? We got in the car and went to Hooters.

And then the next day Justine's water broke.

"I'm ready," Justine said.

Her doctor was on Long Island, but we couldn't get there quick enough so we went to the closest local hospital. Justine delivered our baby, and our baby died. And let me just say right now, I never lost faith in God.

We had never told our family, our children, that there was a problem. We had never told our kids that the baby might not survive because we held on to our faith, our belief, our God, our prayers.

We both held on with everything we had.

When the kids came to the hospital we told them.

I went into the room to be with Justine, and she was distraught—sad and crying and overwhelmed—and how could she not be? Our children were, too; how could they not be?

And so were our fans—folks we didn't even know, but who were living with us weekly on our TV show; how could they not be?

It was an unbearably sad day.

We had decided to share the birth on our TV show, *Run's House,* on MTV, because all of our fans, all of the viewers, were so invested in our daily lives, so invested in our family. They, too, were our family, even though we didn't know them personally. Every single week, they shared our lives, our stories, our home, our family.

The outpouring of love, concern, and generosity was a huge blessing. Cards, flowers, and well wishes filled the room; condolences came in by the bucketful. So much kindness was pouring in. I have a tough shell, an armor that I wear, a form of protection, but my heart was breaking, and cracking open.

I had lost my baby but not my faith, and all I wanted to do, needed to do, had to do, was comfort Justine. That was my main objective. She needed to heal emotionally as well as physically after carrying our baby, Victoria Ann, to term. When we went home, she took to bed to heal.

I needed to surround myself with God, with words of serenity and comfort; find a place where I could refill my hurting soul; a place where I could hear the prayers and let them cradle me, and hold me tight; a place where I could let the prayers in, where I could empty my head and open my heart and hear words.

God's words.

Justine's words.

Joey, I wanna adopt, let's adopt: Justine's words—her voice, her desire, her passion—came roaring back full force. I could hear them in my head.

We set out on that journey.

We started adoption proceedings and were able to adopt a beautiful little baby. She was one month old when she came into our lives, and let me tell you what I know, what I believe: God had a plan, and all those months and mornings that I woke up at five, that I got down on my knees in my crack-of-dawn prayer, was so I could be a better father: more patient, more compassionate, more understanding, more loving.

My prayers did not go to waste.

It's easy to blame God for not answering our prayers; it's easy to get angry and bitter and resentful. But HE had and has bigger plans. There are children who come into this world unwanted, who need to be held and nurtured and nourished and loved, and Justine and I were able to make that happen.

Miley is our miracle.

Justine

(VICTORIA ANN SIMMONS)

"JOEY, I WANNA ADOPT, LET'S ADOPT."

That's what I told Joey.

I told him that I really wanted to adopt a baby.

I don't know why, but I just had that deep in my heart.

Joey and I had two children together, two amazing kids, and I was the stepmom to his three wonderful kids, but adoption was tugging at my heart.

Joey wasn't too keen on that; it wasn't that he didn't think it was a good idea, or a good thing, or a kind thing to do, it was just if we were going to have another baby, he wanted us to at least try and make a baby, and so we stopped using contraceptives and I got pregnant.

We were thrilled.

And then first-trimester morning sickness kicked in.

I would eat and throw up, eat and throw up.

Truthfully, I felt like I was wasting an unbelievable

amount of food. I was eating everything and not keeping it down. You know how women always talk about the weird combination of foods they crave, pickles and ice cream, sushi and bacon? I craved Hooters wings. I craved all kinds of food I wouldn't normally crave, and Joey kept his promise that whatever I craved, whatever food I wanted, he would make sure I got it. But hardly anything stayed down.

I just ate and threw up.

It wasn't until the second checkup that we got some very bad news—heart-wrenching—and the doctor gave us some very hard choices.

We put our faith in God, and we decided to have the baby. We believed that this baby could be and would be a miracle.

After all, miracles do happen.

JOEY WAS GETTING UP every single morning and praying, and he was praying for this baby, our baby, to be healthy. Like clockwork, he would get out of bed and pray for the baby, pray for me, pray for us.

For months and months and months.

And my belly grew bigger, and I, too, prayed for this baby to be a healthy baby. I had heard a wonderful story about a woman who was told that her baby wouldn't survive, and she put her faith in God and in her prayers, and the baby did survive. Not only that, the baby thrived, and thinking of this story got us through some hard times, some scary times. I held on and I prayed on and that's what I prayed for: for our baby to survive and thrive.

We held on until the very last moment.

I DELIVERED OUR BABY, Victoria Ann, and I got to hold her for a few minutes, and then she died.

We lost her.

We were all so very distraught.

Our kids knew nothing about what we were going through; we didn't share the bad news with them until they got to the hospital, and they—like all the viewers and fans who watched our show, *Run's House*—heard that news, and witnessed that birth, along with us.

Our children were deeply sad, so deeply pained. And even though I was so sad, even though my heart was so heavy and breaking into pieces, I was never angry with God.

I truly believed there was a reason for this.

LOSING A BABY IS HARD on a marriage; it's hard on love, it's hard on your body, it's hard on your heart. It's hard on your trust and hard on your faith; it tests you in ways that you aren't prepared for. Even if you're the strongest person in the world, losing a baby shakes you to your core. There's a lot of blame, especially a lot of self-blame, that circulates in your head.

I had carried Victoria Ann full-term; she was in me, a part of me. I could feel her every single day in me.

Joey found comfort in God and being with me.

I found comfort going under the covers.

For the most part, on most days, I was trying to heal my body, heal my sadness, heal my sorrow, and heal my heart.

I cried a lot.

I went through a lot of wondering, *What if?* A lot of waking up in the middle of the night and feeling lonely. I wasn't lonely for Joey; he was right there, comforting me, holding me, loving me strong and good; he was trying so hard to ease me. He was there 100 percent.

I was lonely for my child.

Everything I heard about or read said that women who carry a baby full-term and then lose that baby can still feel that life inside of them. They still feel that baby.

So many questions would swirl around in my head.

But never once, not once, did I question God.

LIFE IS FILLED WITH HARD times and rough times, and rough patches and many tests.

Why? is a question I asked a million times, and then while Joey was lying down next to me in bed, holding me, comforting me, he asked me this *why*: "Why don't we adopt?" Repeating the very same words I had asked him previously.

When he said those words, all my pain melted.

That was what I really wanted to do.

I don't know why, I just did.

It felt absolutely right.

That was God's plan from the beginning; I knew it, I felt it, deep in my soul and in my heart.

Right away I started thinking about how to adopt a baby, and you know how when you put that kind of energy out into the world, the world helps you try to figure out how to make something like that work? Sure enough, folks started helping us. Our kids' teacher at the time had been adopted, and she helped us with all the paperwork, mounds of paperwork, stuff I didn't even know about, and before we knew it we had our baby girl, and we were bringing her home.

She was one month old when we brought her into our lives.

Miley.

There are still times that I forget that I didn't actually carry her, birth her. Miley is as much from my body as Victoria was.

I want all women to know that if they can't conceive a baby or carry a baby, adoption is truly a miracle.

It is.

To be able to give a baby love, to be able to give a baby a home, to be able to give a baby a good life—that's the miracle.

REV'S TAKEAWAYS

- For me, first and foremost was prayer. I prayed: *All will be okay. ALL WILL BE OKAY.*

- Second: Care for each other. Look out for each other. We looked toward each other, at each other, never away from each other.

- This is a very hard time. Carrying a baby full-term and then losing that baby is emotionally and physically and spiritually difficult. Make sure the kids in the family are coping, are dealing with this as a unit; we made sure that all the kids were involved and taken care of.

- Trust in God's plan. We looked toward God. We prayed for strength, for comfort, for wisdom, for what he had planned next for us.

- Another piece of advice we want to give is—when you're ready, because it's a big step—to think about adoption. Think about a baby that will fill your heart. Justine and I both believe that *Adoption Is an Option.*

JUSTINE'S TAKEAWAYS

- At first, I felt very sad, very aware of the pain and the sorrow, and the loss. I recommend that you not push those feelings away or push them down. The enormity of losing a child after carrying it full-term will have a profound effect on you.

- When dealing with grief or any painful loss, I recommend tremendous amounts of self-care and self-love, and compassion.

- There will come a time when the emptiness you feel starts to heal up a bit. We had created a beautiful baby room for Victoria, and what happened was quite miraculous: Joey came in and repeated my exact words back to me: *Let's adopt. Let's adopt a baby.* And the minute he said that, I felt all the pain and all the sadness dissipate. Here's a truth: adoption is not an easy process. It takes fortitude and determination and mounds of paperwork, and it doesn't happen overnight, so patience is required. But just knowing we were now on that track—the track of adopting a baby, my original desire to adopt a baby—gave us hope, and I had something to look forward to. We left the room intact and started adoption proceedings. From the time Victoria passed to the time we adopted Miley was a year.

- If you can't conceive, or if you've had many miscarriages, please consider adopting; it's such a glorious option, and the love is so huge. Like Joey said, *Adoption Is an Option.*

Grown-Up Love

"When I was a child, I spoke as a child, I understood as a child, I thought as a child; but when I became a man, I put away childish things."

1 CORINTHIANS 13:11

Learning to be a grown-up means taking full responsibility for your life and for your relationship. Both people need to put 100 percent into the relationship. That means you're operating on 200 percent. Grown-up love means knowing intimacy is not all about sex, it's about caring for the other person. It's knowing how to forgive—and when to compromise. How sometimes you let the other person win the argument, or let the argument end on its own. Grown-up love also comes when you have children: there are some real big adult lessons that come with becoming parents.

Rev

(DIGGY)

PEOPLE ASK US WHAT CHANGED after we had children.

People ask us what lesson did I learn after we had our first baby.

Well, I'm going to tell you what changed and what lesson I learned, and it's a pretty funny story about a pretty important thing: *learning to take responsibility.*

When Justine gave birth to our first son, Daniel, "Diggy," she had a C-section, which is a pretty serious operation. It meant she needed to stay in the hospital for a few extra days before coming home.

Once she was back home, all she wanted to do was mommy stuff—you know, play with him, cuddle with him, all the stuff that mommies want to do with their newborn babies. She did all of that not knowing that she was supposed to be resting, that her body was still healing from the surgery.

She was supposed to do nothing. Absolutely nothing.

But we didn't know that.

So she did it all. She picked up Diggy, she rocked him, and she sang lullabies to him. It was exhausting—exhausting in the way that having a newborn baby is—but a few days later she became weak and dehydrated, and she was looking and feeling really sick.

So sick she could barely move.

It was just the three of us in the house, and Justine and I realized things had gone pretty wrong, so we called her mom. She freaked out, saying that Justine wasn't supposed to be doing anything. "You were just cut open," she told her. "You just had a C-section—that's a serious operation. You better call the hospital now. Right now."

Mind you, the hospital was all the way out on Long Island, so we ran around like chickens without heads and scrambled to put some stuff together before driving all the way back to the hospital. Diggy was in the back, in a car seat.

When we got there, the nurses got Justine a wheelchair and rushed her right in. They told us Justine was going to be admitted.

I was like, "All right, good, good, okay, admit her, she needs to get healthy and she needs to get better," and I handed Diggy to the nurse.

And the nurse looked at me and said, "What are you doing? You have to keep the baby."

And I said, "What do you mean, I have to keep the baby?

No, you have to take the baby, you have to. I don't know how to take care of this baby. I mean, this here is a baby-baby, this baby is five days old."

The nurse looked at me like I was completely off-the-wall crazy, and she said, "The baby is discharged. We're not taking the baby. YOU need to take care of your baby."

And I was like, "Whoa. Whoa. Back up here. Are you kidding me? Seriously? You're not going to take this baby? What do you want me to do with this baby? I don't know how to take care of this baby. Don't you have a nursery here? Put the baby in the nursery. Let him be with other babies."

The nurse was getting really impatient with me: "Mr. Simmons, you have to take your baby home. He is your baby. We're going to keep your wife for a few days so she can get healthy, so she can get hydrated and strong and start healing, but you need to take that baby home, and you need to take care of your baby."

I was there with a five-day-old baby, and Justine was being rolled into her hospital room, and I was scared to death.

I didn't know what to do. The nurse thought I'd lost my marbles, which I seriously believed I had already lost on the Long Island Expressway driving to the hospital.

I tried one more time to see if they'd let the baby stay in the hospital room with Justine because I was convinced that would be a good thing. I was convinced that I would not be able to take care of the baby, that without Justine at home I would not know what to do, and this way Justine could see her baby every day: all they'd need to do was roll a little baby crib into her room right next to her hospital bed . . . but no such luck.

This was twenty-four years ago. I was thirty years old, and I didn't have a clue what to do.

I called Justine's mom and said, "I got the baby. You told me to take Justine to the hospital, and now I got the baby."

I was ranting about how I couldn't take care of this baby, I had no idea what to do with this baby, I didn't know how to make the milk, and I didn't know anything about Pampers.

She waited until I was finished with my ranting. "Bring him to me," Grandma said. "Just bring him to me."

I did it. And then I went home.

I was back in the house, a big dark, empty house, and feeling like, *What the hell just happened?*

I was also feeling scared, lonely, and a little lost.

Justine was in the hospital.

The baby was across town at Grandma's.

I went back and forth to the hospital every single day to visit Justine, to make sure she was healing. Then I went to Grandma's to see Diggy, who was content and happy because his Grandma knew how to take care of him.

Things were on track.

Justine was getting better, getting healthier, getting her spirit back, Diggy had his grandma and aunts loving him, taking care of him, and I was feeling like there was a light, and not just any light, but a klieg light, at the end of this tunnel.

What changed, what lesson did I learn, what advice would I give?

TAKEAWAYS

- Take responsibility. A baby is going to need you, a baby is going to depend on you, especially if your wife gets sick or something happens so she isn't able to care for that baby. You need to be prepared to deal with whatever comes your way, so make sure you're taking the birthing classes with your spouse, that you know how to swaddle a baby, bottle-feed, all of it.

- Really, I can't stress it enough: be hands-on. Learn how to change a diaper, learn how to bathe your baby, feed your baby. Anything your wife knows how to do, you should, too.

- If you can, hire people to help you. If you can't hire people, if that's not in your budget, reach out to your family and to friends to help you. That's something we learned to do: we learned to ask for help.

Our Blended Family

The definition of a blended family *per Merriam-Webster is*

"a family that includes children of a previous marriage

of one spouse or both."

Rev

I CAME INTO MY MARRIAGE to Justine with three kids from my previous marriage: Vanessa, Angela, and JoJo.

I had them on alternating holidays and every other week.

And let me just say that I hear about a lot of families who really struggle with coming together, with blending together. Kids from one marriage and kids from another marriage who come together and live together and bring a ton of baggage to their new family.

And maybe, just maybe, that baggage comes from a previous marriage that was unloving or filled with unhappiness, and that kind of marriage will always have an effect on the children. Or maybe that baggage comes from one of the parents getting ill and dying and the children are grieving from that massive loss, and maybe that baggage is just a ton of attitude, a ton of not getting along, and they're always fighting.

There is jealousy and there is resentment and there is competition. You got one set of kids who grew up with one set of parents, and then you have another set of kids growing up with another set of parents.

I hear about that all the time: *This kid and that kid don't get along; that stepmother and that kid don't see eye to eye; that stepfather and that son, they don't want to be in the same room.*

It's tough bringing people together, especially when they're your new family and your kids from a different marriage.

Justine

AND ONE THING I WANT TO SAY UPFRONT: if you love someone, but you don't love their kids or want their kids around, or you just want to be married with none of that extra responsibility, with none of the extra "baggage," don't get married. If you love someone who doesn't love your kids and is mean to your kids, DO NOT MARRY THAT PERSON for your own selfish reasons, because your child will suffer either early in life or later on in life from abuse or neglect and God knows what else. If you want to have freedom and be able to go and do and run around and there are kids in the mix . . . do not get married.

I say that with absolute conviction.

Rev

OKAY, BACK TO US, Justine and me, and my kids and our kids, our family.

None of that jealousy, none of that competition, none of that resentment reared its head in our home and in our lives together, either when it was first me and Justine and my kids, or when our family started to grow bigger.

None of that happened because my wife has a heart of gold.

Justine

IN REALITY, Vanessa, Angela, and JoJo were my first kids, who I fell in love with and took care of. I knew them and loved them and took care of them before Diggy, Russy, and Miley were born.

Rev

JUSTINE IS PURE GOODNESS, head to toe, and when I tell you she opened her heart, soul, and arms to and lifted my children, I mean that literally and figuratively. She held them and she took care of them and she loved them like they were her own. That is the absolute truth.

It took a woman with great confidence and great commitment to loving others unconditionally.

That's Justine.

Even her name sounds angelic.

Justine.

Justice.

Just in time.

Just right.

Just perfect.

Just the right woman for me.

Justine.

Justine

THEY'RE GOOD KIDS, I'd tell him.
They're smart kids, I'd boast.
They're kind and generous, I'd say.

Rev

IT TAKES A REAL GOOD WOMAN to want to share all the love. When I say that, what I mean is it takes a real good person—whether it's a woman or a man—to be able to give love freely, to make sure everyone, and I mean everyone, feels wanted and cared for and loved and cherished.

And then we added three more kids to our family. First Diggy. Then Russy. Then Miley.

Welcome to *Run's House*.

HAVING A LOT OF KIDS IN OUR HOUSE meant there was going to be a lot of noise; a lot of TV and games; a lot of playing indoors and playing outdoors; a lot of shouting and screaming and hollering and whooping it up; a lot of messes; a lot of fast food; a lot of crying and a lot of laughing.

A lot of paying attention—making sure all was good, all

was okay, all was going smoothly, all was right in our world with our big blended family.

The other thing that happened in our house, the kids started taking care of each other, and they are still taking care of each other to this day.

Angela would hold Diggy and carry him on her hip.

JoJo would play with Diggy and Russy, and would teach them games and play sports with them. They would sing, dance, rap, and put on performances.

And all the kids—every single one—would carry and play with and hold Miley; she was like a little doll.

OUR KIDS LOVE EACH OTHER.

Our kids like each other.

Our kids protect each other.

They make sure that there is very little competition between them, none of the *he got, she got, why not me got* in our house. And when moments of jealousy and competition—feeling hurt—come up, Justine and I work very hard at making sure all the kids feel equal—equally loved, equally seen, equally heard, equally valued. We never play favorites. It's so important for children to feel and know that they're loved.

When I hear that families don't get along, that kids feel left out or excluded or hurt, or one gets and the others don't, I want to share this wisdom, what I know to be true not just for my family, but for all families that come together: You have to work on it.

DO UNTO OTHERS, THE BIBLE SAYS, *as you would have them do unto you.*

That is our family.

Our big beautiful blended family.

TAKEAWAYS

- Love as much as you would want to be loved.

- Give as much as you would want to be given.

- Take care of others as much as you would want to be taken care of.

- Watch out for each other.

- Stand up for each other. Stand beside and stand for each other. Be good to each other.

- Share and be generous and be kind.

Attentive Love

"Let all that you do be done in love."

1 CORINTHIANS 16:14

Knowing without having to ask. Doing without having to be asked.
Paying attention to the smallest details and the largest details.
Pay attention or they will look for that attention elsewhere.

Rev

(MILEY)

THERE WAS A TIME WHEN my daughter Miley and I had difficulty connecting with each other. She was eleven years old, and there was a bit of distance in our relationship. We were having the toughest time communicating.

I know that's not unusual or unheard of; lots of fathers and daughters have a struggle or go through some stuff at some point in their relationship. When children are growing up, though, they change. So you don't always see what they need right away, and they feel the lack of acknowledgment.

When Miley was a kid, I was caught up in my own world, and the truth is that I wasn't paying attention. I was probably not paying enough attention to a lot of people because I was wrapped up in my own stuff and my own business, and Miley could feel that I was too busy for her.

I'm sure she would ask me something or try to get my attention, and I would just shake my head, as if I were saying, *Not now,* or *I'm too busy,* or I would just brush her off as if to say, *Please, come back later.*

This went on for a while, the lack of closeness, until one day when I needed some love and I tried connecting with Miley, and she said these words to me: *I don't know how we can connect, Dad.*

Whoa.

Talk about a truth hit, talk about a truth bomb.

Those words really hurt my heart. As you can imagine, all of this really hurt Justine's heart, too, because she's all about paying attention to the kids. And of course, my not being present was hurting Miley.

That was all I needed to hear, to get me to perk up, to get me to sit up straighter. I'm always telling folks that they have to turn being selfish into being selfless.

Now it was time for me to walk and talk the walk and talk, so to speak.

Something that I admire so very much in Justine is her selflessness. She has that down to a science. She does it with such grace and ease. It just rolls off her. Easy. She is always making sure that everyone is doing okay.

I wanted to have a loving relationship with my daughter.

I tried to be more attentive, to be more present. I tried. Some days it worked, and some days it didn't, but I wasn't going to give up, I wasn't going to let Miley slip away, and I prayed to God that he would send me what I needed to get back on track with her.

Then, like magic, my prayer was answered.

I don't know how many of you out there watch *Riverdale*, but it's a very popular show, and Miley was completely over the moon, dreamy-eyed about Cole Sprouse, the actor who plays Jughead on the show.

Now, I know all about the *Archie* comics. I know all about Archie and Jughead and Betty and Veronica and Riverdale because I read *Archie* comics when I was a kid. But I didn't know this guy Cole, and now everything, *everything*, was all about Cole.

I'D SAY, "Miley, it's cold outside," and she'd say, "No, Daddy, it's *COLE* outside."

I'd say, "Miley, the refrigerator is cold," and she'd say, "No, Daddy, the refrigerator is *COLE*."

One day about a month before Christmas, she came upstairs to our bedroom and said, "Daddy, can you please get me to meet Cole Sprouse, can you?"

First of all, let me just say, when your daughter looks at you with that beautiful face, those gorgeous eyes, and asks you if you can do something for her, you seriously melt. You are in a puddle.

And second, the arrow went straight into my heart, because she came to me and asked me to do something for her.

That was a breakthrough.

Miley had never asked me for a favor. I know a lot of kids who ask their parents, especially parents who are famous, for favors—tickets to concerts, autographs, stuff like that—but this was the first time ever that Miley had asked me to do something for her. Meeting Cole Sprouse was something she really wanted, and I was not going to let her down.

I wanted to be a hero to my daughter.

Not knowing how in the world I was going to get this done, I figured at least that there was no way that this twenty-six-year-old actor, this guy Cole Sprouse, didn't know about RUN DMC. Surely he had to know about "Walk This Way," surely he had to know about "Christmas in Hollis," surely he knew about rap music.

And surely there was some way that I could get this guy to reach out to my daughter: a text, a card, something. I decided I was going to contact everyone I knew who could help me make this happen, and I went to bed that night saying these words: *It can be done.*

A few days later, after making phone calls and sending texts and asking people if they knew someone who knew someone who knew someone; after hitting a few walls; after a few people said, Yeah, let me see what I can do, Justine came to me and said, "You know who knows Cole Sprouse?"

I'm going to stop here for a second and tell you something about my wife that is just so lovely.

Justine was watching me trying to make this happen and she wanted it to happen just as much as I did, but this was an opportunity for me to make it right with my daughter, so she was going to let me do my thing. She wasn't going to interfere, but after watching me struggle with this a little bit, she came to my rescue. She came without making a fuss because she wanted this for Miley, and she wanted this for my relationship with Miley.

She was cheering me on silently, and then in pure Justine fashion, she said, "You know who knows Cole Sprouse?"

"Who?"

"Phill Lewis."

JUSTINE TOLD ME that Miley said that she saw on social media that Phill Lewis posted about hanging out with Cole Sprouse on the set of *Riverdale*. Phill Lewis played Mr. Moseby on *The Suite Life of Zack & Cody*, and Cole Sprouse played Cody.

Now, this was all becoming a bit mystical, because we knew Phill Lewis from our Netflix show *All About the Washingtons*, and it just so happened, mystically enough, that a month before, I had received a text from Phill wishing me a happy birthday, saying he was thinking of me.

Talk about synchronicity.

Talk about prayers being answered.

I got in touch with Phill, and I asked him if he could do me a favor: to please make me a hero to my daughter.

He didn't make any promises, just said he'd do his best.

That's all you can ask of someone, to do their best.

A day or two before Christmas, I got a message on my phone with a video with *Merry Christmas* as the subject.

I clicked on the video, and it was none other than Cole Sprouse with a message for Miley Simmons:

Miley, this is Cole Sprouse here in Los Angeles. I hope you're doing well, from your loving family here in Los Angeles.

You would have sworn that Miley had swallowed the sun while she was watching that video.

TAKEAWAYS

- Never think you can't do something, or accomplish something, or create some magic for your child. Nothing is impossible.

- Be open to stepping out of your comfort zone.

- To be a hero to your child, to show them through your actions, your deeds, that they mean the world to you, is such a great gift. And even though being a hero will fill you with incredible courage, it is a gift that gives them courage as well. Every child wants to believe a parent is made of a little bit of magic.

- Heroism is very often earthbound; it is saying yes, I can do this; yes, I will do this, yes, I will make this happen for you.

You know it's Old School Love when we're wearing Tommy Hilfiger and a football jersey.

Our very happy wedding day! This picture shows the gorgeous bride with Angela, Vanessa, and her mother by her side.

Justine greeting family members at our wedding reception.

"You may give the bride cake . . ."

First time "mommy"
Justine at the baby shower
for Diggy.

Deacon and Deaconess Joseph and
Justine Simmons with baby Diggy.

Us celebrating
the absolute
joy of our baby
Miley's arrival
during a *People*
magazine
photoshoot.

Todd Plitt,
Getty Images

A very debonair Justine's dad in front of the house—just chillin' in a suit!

Ain't nothing like family! Justine and my dad, Daniel Simmons Sr., having a great time at Thanksgiving dinner.

Chillin' with the family in the backyard. Justine is feeding Diggy while we're all hanging with Justine's sister, Leslie.

Diggy hanging out with Mom and Dad.

"What's goin' on here?" Miley looking at Russy and me in the back of a limo while we're both on our cell phones. LOL.

"Who wants this coloring book?" Angela, JoJo, and Diggy having a great time at Diggy's second birthday party.

Vanessa, Angela, JoJo, Diggy, Russy, Justine, and Rev at a Phat Farm Halloween party.

The whole *Run's House* crew at the Kids' Choice Awards.

Albert L. Ortega, Getty Images

The whole *Run's House* crew . . . on the red carpet!

Dimitrios Kambouris, Getty Images

Good love, amazing love,
grand love—at the Grand Wailea
in Maui on our wedding
anniversary.

Having a blast in a helicopter.
Never gonna let you go!

All smiles while celebrating our love in Maui.

Cookin' one of Rev Run's Sunday Suppers in the kitchen!
Alexander Tamargo, Getty Images

Justine serving up her famous lasagna . . . with a side of love.
New York Daily News, Getty Images

On the red carpet for the RUN DMC Grammy Lifetime Achievement Award presentation. *Kevin Mazur, Getty Images*

On the Orange Carpet for the Nickelodeon 20th Annual Kids' Choice Awards. *Jesse Grant, Getty Images*

Powerful Love

"Love is patient, love is kind. It does not envy, it does not boast, it is not proud. It does not dishonor others, it is not self-seeking, it is not easily angered, it keeps no records of wrongs."

1 CORINTHIANS 13:4–8

Nothing can stop it or get in its way. It's a magnet, a shooting star, a comet; it's the brightest sun and the fullest moon. It is fierce and mighty, the superhero of love.

Justine

(REV AS A GOOD DAD)

I'M NOT JUST SAYING Joey is an amazing father because he's my husband and the father of our children; he really is amazing. He's so kind. He's so generous, and in all the important ways: with his time, his wisdom, and his heart.

He pays attention. He listens. He gets involved. He gives 100 percent. He cares deeply. He really wants to make things work, to make things better, to do the right thing for his kids and his relationship with them. He wants to know what the kids are doing, what the kids are thinking, how the kids are feeling. He genuinely wants to know that they're doing okay and feeling okay, and that the world is treating them well.

I think having the life Joey had when he was younger—all the fame, all the recognition, all the attention, all the money, all the things—made him so much more compassionate, so much more understanding, so much more tolerant. It made him not only want to be a role model for his kids, but for all kids trying to figure out who they are, what they want.

He knows what it's like to be the center of attention, to be a shining star, to shine so brightly it can be blinding, and then to wake up one day and realize he wanted so much more out of life than that, and by "more" I mean finding God. That changed Joey's life. When Joey found God he found joy, peace, happiness; he found himself.

He found that his worth was more than what was in his bank account. He found that his value was more than gold or platinum records.

He's so proud of his kids, and he shows them, he tells them, he lets them know. That is so important in a child's life, to be told how good they are, how well they're doing, to be told how proud you are of their accomplishments, and he's very proud of the way they handle all their struggles and disappointments and bad days. He learned that from his own father, who was also supportive and attentive.

He loves each one of his children, all six of them, with all of his heart, and they know that. They see that. His actions speak volumes.

One other thing that most people don't know about Joey is how open and accepting he is.

When Vanessa became pregnant and she wasn't married, she was so worried that her dad would be unhappy with that. She was scared he would disapprove—because he's a reverend and so many people, millions of people, know him and follow him, and because she didn't want to disappoint him.

There are so many parents who would be angry, upset, who would turn their back on their daughter, who would be pushing their daughter to get married, but not Joey. He accepted her and her decision to have the baby. He was happy for her, and told her that whatever she needed he would be there, that we would be there, both of us, for her.

The same thing with Angela, when she became pregnant and she wasn't married . . . and the same thing with JoJo when his fiancée got pregnant—Joey was loving and compassionate and accepting, open and caring.

I am so proud of Joey and how he is with our kids, how he shows them through his actions and his words and his faith and his massive and open heart the irrefutable power of love.

TAKEAWAYS

- Pay attention to your children, listen to their needs and their wants, listen to their pain, be kind when they're suffering, be understanding when they're feeling sad, offer a shoulder not a lecture when they need reassurance.

- Try to not react immediately when they come to you with a problem; most kids don't want to be talked at, they want to be heard.

- Really listen to the words they're saying to you; sometimes what's not said, what's not spoken, is much louder and much more important than what is.

- Children need praise when they've done something wonderful.

- Before you criticize: compliment—give them kudos, and praise them. That will stay with them for a lifetime.

Romantic Love

"Love does not delight in evil but rejoices with the truth. It always protects, always trusts, always hopes, always perseveres. Love never fails."

1 CORINTHIANS 13:6–7

Candles, champagne, moonlit walks on a beach, dancing in the dark, a corner table in a favorite restaurant. Holding her or his hand just because. Brushing her hair out of her eyes. Locking your arm in his. Little love notes. Post-its that say I love you. Poems filled with compliments and beauty. Little gifts, trinkets, for no reason at all. Flowers by the handful . . . or a vase full. Romantic love: It's private. It's sexy. It's just the two of us . . .

Rev

(DO WHAT YOU LOVE)

MY WIFE AND I HAVE many hobbies that we do together. Three of them became a massive part of our lives and a big part of our success: cooking, traveling, and renovating.

We approach the things we love to do together with pure love and genuine passion. I think because we do things that way—without strings attached, without expectation—that it's pure. That's how we ended up with three shows on network TV at the same time.

It started with a phone call about doing a renovation show on the DIY/HGTV channel, which ultimately was named *Rev Run's Renovation*. You could have knocked us over. They offered us a deal to do a show about renovating *our house*. Let me tell you, our house really needed some renovation; it had a lot of wear and tear. All of those years were starting to show up on the walls, on the floors.

You can just imagine that Justine was over-the-moon excited about shopping for appliances and furniture and tables and chairs and rugs and cabinets and . . . If you've seen the show, you already know how much Justine loves shopping.

We were so hot, the Cooking Channel called with an idea for a show, and after some back and forth, we created a second show, called *Rev Run's Sunday Suppers*.

Justine loves to cook.

A marriage made in culinary heaven.

When you do what you love, when you are kind to other people, work hard, and just let things unfold without wondering what the outcome will be, magic happens. Between your passion and your imagination, anything is possible.

Just to give you an idea how this all went down, at the same time we were renovating our house, the Cooking Channel was trying to get into our house so we could film *Rev Run's Sunday Suppers*. So, we designed the kitchen on the renovation show and the cooking show used that design from the renovation show, which started promoting the cooking show with our brand-new beautiful kitchen, which was being designed on the renovation show.

To say this was a dream come true for Justine and me would be an understatement. Justine was in heaven. And watching her being happy, well, that just fills me to the brim.

Next thing we did was go to the network upfronts.

For those who don't know what the upfronts are, the networks put together all their upcoming shows and they promote them. It's a big deal. We're talking rooms filled with people—everyone from celebrities to actors and network executives. Basically, you see all of the folks involved with all of the upcoming shows.

We met with the president of HGTV and with the president of its network, Scripps Networks Interactive, and they told us that the renovation show was such a success that it was going to go into a second season.

We were just off-the-charts thrilled; we were literally beaming.

Through all the crazy stuff going on, we saw a big stand, a big sign: THE TRAVEL CHANNEL.

So, we thought, why not? We decided to mosey on over to talk to them, because we love to travel. Why not go for three? After all, third time is the charm.

We told an executive at the stand that we had this idea for a romantic travel show: "You know, people need romance; they need to see people being romantic, people traveling around with their wife or their husband, their partner, going to romantic places. Doesn't that sound like a great idea for a TV show? *Rev Run's Romantic Travels*?" And then I added, "Because I think I can inspire men to be more romantic with their wives."

Okay, I'm pretty sure I oversold the romantic part.

The executive told us that he wasn't so sure that their audience would want to see that kind of show; that their audience was more into adventure travel, and we all know Justine and I are not going to be doing rock climbing or mountain climbing or kayaking.

Put me in water and I'm happy. Doesn't matter if it's a pool or a Jacuzzi or the ocean. Put me near any body of water, and I'm as happy as a clam, because clams love water, but no, thank you, to rock climbing.

We let it go, but before we left for the day, I said to the executive, "Hey, if you have any ideas that we might be good for, to be part of your travel shows, we're more than open to hearing about them . . . you know . . . *Rev Run's Travel Show . . .*"

Thinking that nothing would come of this, we left and we were happy. We had two shows on the air, and life was good. We were getting to do what we loved, and we loved what we were doing.

A few days later, we got a phone call from the same Travel Channel executive that we met at the upfronts, and he wanted to pitch us a travel show idea.

It was all about having a plane ticket, one plane ticket, that would take us all the way around the world. We'd fly to Italy, and from there we'd get to fly to another city, and then we'd keep going to other places from there. The whole deal was that it's cheaper flying to all these amazing places, all these cool cities and destinations, on *one* ticket.

The best part was that we could take our kids with us. We could all travel the world together.

We said yes. *Let's do it. Yes.*

Cooking is fun at home. Renovating your whole entire home on television is fun and it is fabulous.

But nothing, nothing, is more fabulous than traveling the entire world, and that's what the network was offering us, to travel the entire world with the people we love the best.

That is called a grand slam.

I'm like . . . *whoa, whoa . . . what is going on?*

How were we going to do three shows?

But we did them. The three things we love to do the most we were now doing on television.

We traveled the entire world in one year, and we had a ball. We went to Japan and China and Dubai and Mexico and Jamaica and Thailand and Denmark and Amsterdam and Italy. That one ticket took us everywhere you could possibly think of. The show was called *Rev Runs Around the World*.

All of our hobbies, which we would do if no one was watching us or looking at us or paying us for, turned into dream projects.

And I know that there are folks out there who think, *Well, you're Rev Run, you're famous, you got clout, you were a big, huge rapper and you're a well-known reverend and you're out there, and it's easy to be offered this kind of stuff, all these dream projects, when you're a star or a celebrity . . .*

But here's the truth, here is what I absolutely believe: when you're not doing something with the expectation that it should be handed to you, or it should be given to you because of who are, the entire world opens up to you. It happens because of the love you pour into what you're doing.

If you're in tune with God, and if you're in tune with each other, if you're full of joy and not complaints, if you're full of gratitude and appreciation, not *where's mine, where's mine, gimme . . . gimme . . . gimme;* if you're full of adventure and curiosity and wonder, if you're full of intention—if you're single-mindedly seeking—what you love to do will become how you love living your life.

Again, the world is filled with magic.

We are proof of that.

Justine

(DO WHAT YOU LOVE)

I CAN TELL YOU how much I love cooking and how much I love renovating and decorating and how much I love traveling, but I'm sure Joey covered all those bases.

But I want to tell you about what I love to do most, and what I love most. Joey knows—actually, everybody knows, because it is not a secret—that I love, love, love Christmas.

I love everything about Christmas. From the decorations to the songs to the colors to the food to the kindness, the generosity, the compassion—the charity—that feels and seems boundless, the whole season brings me so much joy. One of the great joys is giving back to others, giving to those who have less. I love the spirit of Christmas, and how opening the boxes of decorations each year reminds me of all the years before when we opened those boxes. Every time I see those gorgeous glass balls and figurines—all of our special mementos—I think of our first years together as a couple, as a family. I think of everything we've built, and everything that is yet to come.

I love Christmas so much that I wish it could be every day, all year-round.

So, Joey and I, we have a ritual.

We put up our tree usually two months before Christmas, and then I slowly add other things to the house every day. I try to jazz up the piano by putting a runner on it topped with glass jars filled with sparkly lights or sparkly balls and framed photos, or I'll hang an elegant candelabra with beautiful colored tapered candlesticks, to add something a bit bold and beautiful to keep the Christmas spirit expanding and growing. And a lot of times I'll go out, and Joey will come with me, to buy and to add just a few new things to put on the tree along with all the old familiar ornaments.

We always add a little something new to our Christmas tree and tradition.

I love Christmas and I love to go shopping, and those two things go really well together. Okay, they go perfectly together.

Joey always decorates the outside of the house, and he always has that all together by his birthday, November 14. I know he'll get that all taken care of before it's time to celebrate his big day.

He'll put up a few huge wreaths on the front doors and then decorate them all with beautiful Christmas lights. These add a perfect glow, and the house always looks so beautiful, so joyous, from the outside. It's a lot of fun for him to do, because he likes how everybody can see how much care we take in getting ready for the holiday, getting into the spirit of things.

We put the artificial tree up in our living room, and because the ceilings are really high, our tree is really, really tall.

It takes maybe three days to decorate the entire tree because I like to take my time. I want it to look gorgeous. I want all the ornaments to hang on the tree branches perfectly, beautifully, and magically. I'll add something, step back, and look to see if it works, if it looks right. If there's a hole that needs to be filled or a space that's too cluttered, then I'll add more. And now after all these years, I even let the kids help decorate the tree without me being too interfering, too controlling. Before, I never let them decorate without breathing down their necks, telling them what to do and where to put stuff. For many years they would be putting up decorations and ornaments and ribbons and I would be telling them *no, no, not there . . . there . . . over there . . .* I wanted everything, every single little thing, in a certain place and even though they didn't say anything, I know they didn't like my being pushy. Well, actually, they did say something; they told me that they didn't like me telling them what to do, and really, what kid likes it when their parents are pushy? But I don't do that anymore. I learned my lesson. So now I let the kids do their thing, and they love it. And of course, I'll fuss with the tree when they're not looking, but not too much. They love the way the tree turns out.

And it's funny because when I was younger, when we were kids, my parents always let us decorate the tree and they never interfered.

I love Christmas so much that we even keep the tree up for months and months, much to Joey's dismay, although he's a good sport about all of it. He knows how much it means to me.

Like on Valentine's Day, I'll do pink hearts and red balls and all sorts of pretty decorations. One year we even made it to Easter, putting little bunnies and egg-shaped ornaments on the tree. I think that was the year Joey put his foot down and said, "Let's not keep the tree up that long," so we don't do "Easter" Christmas trees anymore.

I think what I love most about Christmas is that it seems to bring out the best in people—it's a true time of giving. It feels so magical; seeing everything lit up and glowing during this season adds so much joy to people's lives.

REV'S TAKEAWAYS

- Find things that you love to do together and schedule time to do them. Find the things that bring you closer, bring more intimacy; find the things you like to share.

- Plan a romantic getaway and explore together. Whether it's a big vacation or a day trip to a nearby town you've always wanted to explore, that quality one-on-one time is a great way to bring some romance—some magic—back into your relationship.

- Try new things. Even if it's not for you but something your partner loves. An open heart brings a lot of joy, and joy multiplies. You'll be surprised how many things you find that you actually like doing together once you open your heart.

- Don't be afraid to be adventurous; try something completely off the beaten path or out of your comfort zone. Adventures often create the very best memories and the best photo-worthy moments.

JUSTINE'S TAKEAWAYS

- Holidays are a time to give and to be generous in all ways. They are a time to buy a stranger a cup of coffee and bring clothes to a shelter, to donate to charities and organizations and to be philanthropic. They are a time to think of those who don't have, those who are without, and to share. They are a time to bring your own family together, to set aside some differences. A time to put away the past and rekindle the present.

- Special occasions are filled with opportunities to love better, to be kinder and more open-hearted, and create great meals and extraordinary memories.

- Think of a special memory you have from a holiday season—what is it? Can you think of ways to be more generous and giving in your daily life?

- Set resolutions as a family. It's great to teach your children about giving and charity early on, and setting resolutions as a group keeps you accountable in the coming year.

Old School Love

PART ONE

"*Do to others as you would have them do to you.*"

LUKE 6:31

It's all types of love with nostalgia and time as an add-on. It's looking into someone's eyes and not at your cell phone. It's taking a photo and having it last a lifetime, not just an Insta. It's a five-course meal, not fast food. It is waiting for the bus, riding a train, taking your time. It's remembering what she or he looked like when you first laid eyes on them. It is a million questions starting with: Do you remember when? It's growing old together, and growing wiser together, and growing in love together. It's looking back at the people who have inspired you, and made you someone ready and willing to take on this kind of love.

Rev

(MY DAD IS MY GREATEST HERO/ MY DAD WAS MY GREATEST HERO)

DANIEL SIMMONS SR.,
AUGUST 21, 1923–JUNE 12, 2006

ALL KIDS NEED PEOPLE THEY CAN LOOK UP TO, people they want to grow up to be like. They need a mentor who wants them to succeed beyond their own successes and their own wildest dreams, to succeed beyond their own accomplishments.

I believe the definition of a mentor is someone who wants you to exceed their greatness.

My father made sure we were cared for, that we laughed, that we knew the names of everyone in the neighborhood. He was the kind of dad who paid attention, and the kind of dad who made us pay attention, too. If God is in the details, then my dad most certainly pointed me in that direction.

I loved sports as a kid, especially basketball, and I most loved Julius Erving, aka Dr. J. I thought I was Dr. J as a kid, or at the very least that I'd be the next Dr. J, so my dad bought me a shirt that said *Dr. Joey* on it. Dr. J had just changed his number from thirty-two to six, and my dad made sure that the number six was on the back of my shirt.

He worked two jobs so his kids could have the best life possible; he was an attendance supervisor during the day, and he taught a college course, black history, at Pace University at night. Even as hard as he worked, as many hours as he put in—he STILL put up a basketball court in the yard so I could play.

He wanted us to understand that life could be hard and brutal, and he didn't shy away from reminding us that life could throw a curveball, and we needed to pay close attention and be ready to catch it. This was important because during the time I was growing up in Hollis, Queens, there was a lot of unease brewing, with an increase in violence and drugs.

He was funny—funny *and* witty—and he loved to make everyone laugh. He knew everyone in the neighborhood and everyone knew him. But more than anything, he taught me how to be present in someone's life, 100 percent fully present.

That's really important for a kid. There are a lot of dads who, even though they're living at home, just show up on occasion. Either they're working too hard and they have no time for their own life or they're drinking too hard or they're gallivanting around, hanging out with their friends or with women. Being present makes a huge difference. No matter what, my dad was always there, rooting me on. Being my champion.

When I was a kid, there was a period of time when my mom and dad separated for a little while, and on Valentine's Day he sent me a card with five dollars in it.

Opening our mailbox and seeing an envelope addressed to me, Joey Simmons—my heart burst. Here I was, this little kid, and my dad was telling me and showing me that he loved me.

He was always doing stuff like that: giving little gifts and small surprises, sending cards, leaving little toys. The kind of toys you could get at a Woolworth's or a candy store. I know this sounds like a cliché, but it really felt like Christmas a lot of the year in our house. That really rubbed off on me. It's something I do now, always getting Justine and the kids little gifts, doing something special just because. My dad showed me the importance of doing those small gestures, that they make a huge difference.

He was so attentive, he wasn't afraid to show people how much he cared, how much he loved, how much they meant to him; that's who he was, and that is what is embedded, ingrained, deep in me, soul-deep in. It is what I wanted to give all my fans as Run, and what I want to give to all those who follow me as Rev Run.

We were still living in Queens when the first RUN DMC record came out, and many nights we would go to this place called Jamaica Avenue, or The Ave. Two of our songs were on the radio—"Sucker M.C.'s" and "It's Like That"—and they were playing our music all the time at the different neighborhood stores.

There was this one store there, it was a real cool clothing store, a little too pricey for kids from Hollis. But now I had some money in my pocket and I had some extra bounce in my walk and I was going to buy some clothes at this very cool store. I went in, and the sales guy came over to me, and I could tell he knew who I was. We made some small talk, and he told me that my dad had been in the store the week before, telling everyone that his son was Run of RUN DMC.

There I was, standing in the middle of this store, and I felt so overwhelmed with pride that my dad was so freakin' proud of *me*. That meant way more than the money or the clothes.

He would tell everyone, and I mean everyone, that his son was Run of RUN DMC. Shop owners, folks on the bus, anyone and everywhere. He would go into stores, even into the dry cleaners, and brag about me, about my accomplishments.

Here is something I want folks to know: his being proud of me made me prouder of me. When you see your own father light up, shine up, you can't help but catch some of the light, some of that shine. You can't help but want to be shinier and brighter.

That's what a mentor does: they want you to shine up, shine bright, to be as huge as you can be in the world.

And let me tell you something else: my dad, now, he was a true poet. I realized early on where I got my love of poetry from, my love of words from, my love of rapping from.

He even wrote a few of the songs on our albums, some of our biggest hits.

"Proud to Be Black," one of our huge hits, featured his lyrics. Those words helped make our *Raising Hell* album explode.

He was the life of every party. When I say that, I mean he was big and bold and gregarious and he made everyone feel loved, he made everyone feel important. He made sure that you were noticed, seen, and heard. You know that saying, *Children should be seen and NOT heard*? Well, my dad believed children should be seen AND heard.

He had strong ethics.

Strong values.

If he believed in something, he fought for it.

He marched for justice and peace, and he stood up for the things and for the people he believed in.

He fought hard for black people, the underprivileged, the voiceless; he fought hard for civil rights and human rights, for human dignity.

To this day when I think of my dad, I think about all that he gave me, showed me, taught me, ingrained in me; he instilled that sense of values, that sense of goodness, that sense of right and wrong, in me.

And he saw me.

And when I say he saw me, I mean he really saw me. He saw me as his son, his child; he saw me as Run, as a rapper, a DJ, a performer; he saw me as a husband, a father; and later on, he saw me as Rev Run.

And he was proud of me, so proud of who I became.

Yes, my dad was my hero. And I am proud of him, who he was, his legacy.

And I am so very proud to be his son.

Justine

(ROLE MODELS)

GROWING UP I WAS FORTUNATE to have a few amazing mentors in my life, both women and men, who I admired and respected and looked up to and loved.

When I was in my teens, I worked for a couple—Mr. and Mrs. Burnett—at their luggage and handbag store out on Long Island. They both had such a strong work ethic. They were kind and caring, and impeccable in word and in deed, and they treated me with such respect.

When people put their trust in you, when they see something in you that maybe you don't see in yourself, it is so important to live up to that expectation and belief, to that trust. They gave me all of that, and that was a huge gift.

And then there's Bishop Bernard Jordan and his wife, Pastor Debra, who have been two very important and vital examples in my life. Their devotion to God and their love and respect for each other is so inspiring, so encouraging; so life-giving and so life-affirming.

As far as family relationships go, I'd have to say my mom and my stepdad were my greatest mentors. I knew what love was, what it could be and should be, watching them. They taught me about good love, kind love, gentle love, and compassionate love.

When I think of the three women in my life who had the biggest impact on me, who had the greatest effect on me—those three women are my nana, my stepmom, Daisy, and my mom.

My nana, my mother's mother—my grandma—was definitely one of my first real role models. She pretty much helped raise me as a little girl. She was a woman of deep faith, and she taught me to be kind and generous. She showered me with kindness and compassion, and she also had tremendous patience, which I came to understand is truly a great virtue.

When I was a little girl, I was most definitely a bit of a tomboy. I loved hanging with the boys and playing football, running with the ball and getting down in the dirt. But I was also a real girly girl. I loved girly things. Frilly things. So my nana would take me to Woolworth's, and she would buy me cute clothes and cute underwear and cute barrettes for my hair that were glittery and sparkly, and then we would have lunch at the counter, just me and her.

I'll always cherish those days, and the things she did for me, like doing my hair up on school days. Even now, I love getting my hair done, trying different styles.

She taught me how to do jigsaw puzzles, and we would do them together. To this day, I love doing jigsaw puzzles.

She was neat and tidy and so organized, and yes, you guessed it: so am I. I love straightening our drawers and cleaning out our closets and having things all tidy and neat in our house, and that just gets Joey all nuts. He'll come home from being away on a trip, and he'll walk into our bedroom and the entire closet—every single piece of clothing, and all the shoes, and all the handbags and belts—will be pulled out and strewn everywhere, while I rearrange everything from the big drawers to the hangers to the little drawers, for a complete makeover.

And my nana, she loved having a routine; that was really important to her. She liked having order in her life, everything in its place. She would make breakfast at the same, exact time every single morning, and she would make supper—it wasn't "dinner," it was "supper"—at the same, exact time every evening. And she would watch her TV shows at a certain time every single night.

I learned to be disciplined because of her, and I believe I inherited many of her other fine qualities.

Then there was Daisy.

When my mom and dad got divorced, I went to live with my dad. At that time Daisy was his girlfriend. I was very close to my dad. He supported me; he supported my love for music and my love for singing, and he supported me when I liked to play sports, my being a tomboy and all, and he was just fun to be around.

I wasn't really sure about Daisy at first; maybe it was because she was his girlfriend and being a girlfriend meant, or felt like, it wasn't permanent, so getting attached to someone who may or may not be in your life every day was a bit iffy. But Daisy stayed and I grew to really like her. Then I grew to really love her, and she brought stability and organization into my life. She was like Nana in that way. Being a teenager, stability and organization are good things to be around.

I look back now and I can see why God had me live with my dad.

I was the only one who went to live with him; my sisters stayed with my mom, and I truly believe that God pulled me to live with my dad because Daisy taught me about being responsible. She was very stern but she was also soft-spoken, gentle, and she was beyond loving.

I'm absolutely sure, 100 percent, that Daisy helped me embrace all of my stepchildren because she embraced and loved me unconditionally, and for that I will always be indebted to her.

Then there's my mom.

My mom was one of the bravest women I've ever known. I would even go so far as to say she is a superhero role model.

My mom had breast cancer, and she had one breast removed, a mastectomy. And still, she fought that with every fiber of her being.

She had stomach cancer and pancreatic cancer, and still, she fought those with every fiber of her being.

She had liver cancer and fought that with every fiber of her being.

She was a cancer survivor, and she came out stronger and braver and more determined each and every single time.

She was filled with unbelievable courage. In my eyes, she was not just a survivor, she was a *thriver*.

She had so much strength and courage, so much faith and wisdom, and she was filled with boundless hope.

I am so immensely grateful that I have had, and still have, women in my life who are fighters, champions; women who are so determined to live their life fully, with dignity and strength and grace and the love of God.

Women who, when they come up against odds and obstacles and were facing their own mortality, they beat the odds; women who come out of those challenges stronger and braver and more beautiful, more dignified, much wiser for the wear.

I believe that growing up around Mr. and Mrs. Burnett and their trust in me taught me about self-esteem and self-respect.

Being with my nana and her showering me with goodness and kindness and love taught me about unconditional love.

Living with Daisy and her compassion and generosity taught me about the power of selflessness.

Watching my mom being brave and courageous and so very strong in the face of adversity taught me about determination and perseverance, never giving up.

Witnessing Bishop Jordan and his wife, Pastor Debra, and their loving God showed me what faith means: faith in God, faith in oneself, faith in others.

Through all of their actions and all of their words, all of their faith and all of their determination—all of their unconditional love—they showed me what real role models and mentors look like and behave like, what real role models and mentors are made of.

I want all girls to have the kind of role models in their lives that I did. I want all women to have mentors who show them what true power is, what good power is, what strong power is—*soft power.* And that soft power—dignity and grace and integrity and compassion—comes from the heart. And pure, unconditional love is what heals, nourishes, inspires us and the world we live in.

TAKEAWAYS

- The people who inspired you as a kid, who made you want to be better as an adult: try to remember what it was they instilled in you.

- It's important to think about the qualities of the people you admire, and ask yourself what you could be doing more of—or doing better—in your own life to let those same qualities shine out, and become a role model for others.

- Show up for your kids. Make time for them every day, and show them you support them. Share your mistakes and foibles because that is how you teach hope, and give others the opportunity to know they are not alone.

- Even if you're working hard, if you only have a few minutes before bed to catch up and hear about their day, don't miss that time. They'll cherish those memories for the rest of their lives—and believe me, you will, too.

- Being a mentor really means being a role model, leading by example, showing the way. It's the core principle of Old School Love.

Old School Love

PART TWO

Rev

(DOING LOVE WELL)

THIS IS A VERY IMPORTANT ISSUE in any relationship: Loving well. Loving smart.

If you love someone well and smart, you will work out all the kinks. You'll learn to become a bit less selfish and a bit more selfless.

It's complicated and it's tough. It's much easier to turn your back and walk out. It's much easier to throw your hands up and get belligerent and start a screaming match. It's much easier to put the blame on the other person and make them feel that it's all their fault and that they're wrong and you're right.

Being righteous, walking away, closing a door, throwing your hands up, giving up . . . that's all easy to do. Working through conflict—well, that's hard work.

My thought is always this: *Marriage is not so much gazing*

into each other's eyes but more looking in the same direction, being on the same page.

That, and turning to God, is the key in our marriage.

Justine and I recently had a disagreement concerning a fashion project that Justine wanted to do and the people she wanted to partner with.

I can tell you straight out that this was not the first time Justine and I had butted heads in a situation like this, but it was the right time for me to learn this lesson once and for all, to not be so arrogant that I would let this kind of dis-agreement rear its head again.

So, bear with me, and you'll see where I finally learned the lesson, and this is a good one for all married couples.

I noticed that Justine didn't want to tell me about what she was working on, and I kept asking her, *Hey, what are you do-ing, what's going on, need any help?* And she hated that. She felt like I was intruding on her project. I could tell this was not a Joey project, or a Justine and Joey project; this was a Justine project, 100 percent hers, and Joey was being a pest.

She finally told me what she was working on and I could tell that she did not want my opinion, she did not want my two cents, she did not want me sticking my nose in her busi-ness. I have very strong opinions, and she wanted no part of them.

I was being a distraction . . . not a helper.

Here's a truth, and I say this because when you know the truth about yourself, it's good to stand in it, to own it.

I wanted to help her without having to ask. I wanted to help her without having to pester her. I wanted her to *invite* me to help her, to hold her hand, to help her through some of her frustration, to give her answers, to give her my opinion about what I thought about her work. I wanted to make her life easier. I wasn't at all comfortable with pushing her and prodding her and pestering her because I wanted her to invite me in.

And here's another major dose of truth: I wanted to be wanted. I wanted to be needed. I saw Justine struggling, and I volunteered to pitch in and help her move things along, but she wasn't having it.

Not one bit.

So, I stopped popping my head in every five minutes, and let her work through her struggles, because I knew that my popping in and out, being annoying, wasn't making it easier for her.

I had to control my impulse to help her. Not easy for a guy like me, wanting everything to go smoothly, beautifully, easily, for Justine.

I went on about my business, and let Justine try to figure out all the things she needed to go on about her business. And every so often, I would check in and watch her trying to figure out how to fix the printer and getting all frustrated, but I had learned and I knew that she did not want me in her business. So, I'd check on her, and then mosey on along.

I was watching my wife—my partner, my best friend, my lover—struggling with a project that she had so much passion for. I saw myself as a concerned husband, partner, and best friend. But the way I was handling it, she saw me as an intrusion.

How did I resolve this conflict?

I stopped doing the stuff that made her nuts.

Again, that is not very easy for a guy like me. But I had to see that my pushing only agitated her. My prodding only made her feel like she was incapable of doing this on her own, figuring it all out on her own. My sticking my head in and out and saying, *Hey, what's up?* wasn't endearing me to her.

It hurts my heart to see the people I love struggling, even if it's struggling with something like a printer that's not working.

So here's what I did.

I took her out to dinner, and I didn't bring up her project and she didn't bring up her project. Because this is the other thing I have learned: the more you pound a nail, the more you beat a dead horse, the more you drive something into the ground—the more you dig yourself deeper into trouble.

We had a lovely dinner and a lovely evening.

The next day I headed out to do some errands.

I was driving around town, going to the strip mall, going in and out of stores, doing my business, picking up things for the kids, for the house, and then I was in CVS walking the aisles looking for some vitamins or something like that when my cell phone rang, and it was Justine.

"Hey, Joey," she said. "Do you want to take me over to Staples?"

She needed me.

Do you know how that made me feel? Like a million bucks.

I rushed right home and picked her up, and I took her straight to Staples, where she got all her stuff taken care of.

Let me tell you what that situation taught me, what that situation showed me.

I thought I was being kind and generous and giving. I thought wanting to help her and take care of her while she was struggling with all of this would be welcomed with open arms, and kisses, and *thank you thank you thank you,* and more kisses and more love.

Justine saw me as not giving her the space she needed to work through her own obstacle course. She saw me badgering her, which made her feel like I was intruding on *her project,* a project that gave her tremendous joy and fulfillment. She saw me as being nosy, not curious.

She saw me as wanting to interfere with her thing, her work.

And when I gave her the space that she needed to work on her project and through whatever bumps she was hitting in this obstacle course, when I stopped being annoying and pestering and pushy, when I went about my own business and left the house and did my thing . . . she let me in, she asked me to help her, she *wanted* my help.

That's when Justine told me, "I know you just wanted to support me, Joey, I know that, and I love you so much for that."

Justine

(DATE NIGHT)

WHEN WE GO OUT ON A DATE I make sure that I feel sexy. I *want* to feel sexy. Date nights, by definition, should be romantic; they should have an extra side, a heaping, of excitement to them. There should be thought and care put into a date night. And by date night, I don't mean a movie and dinner at Cracker Barrel; I mean a romantic place where holding hands comes with the territory.

We start by picking a place that we both love, maybe one that has some great memories, or maybe just a restaurant with a booth in the back corner where we find ourselves easing toward each other after dinner.

When Joey and I go out on a date, I jazz myself up and wear something special. When I do that it almost feels like when we were first dating. There's something about that little added touch: spraying on my favorite perfume (not just my everyday one) and wearing sexy underwear (not just comfy, everyday underwear).

Knowing that it's just going to be the two of us in one of our special places is romantic and intimate in itself. It's exciting. It's kind of like we're sneaking away, sneaking out.

Plus, we get to flirt, and I love flirting with Joey. Honest to God, flirting with Joey is so sexy, and it makes me feel like we're brand-new, and that is just so romantic. Really, it gives me goose bumps just thinking about it.

When we go to a special event, like the Grammys or the Emmys, or some fancy black-tie gala event, I have a personal stylist, and his name is, you guessed it . . . Rev Run, aka Joey Simmons.

Joey Simmons is my personal stylist.

And I really like that. Joey loves picking out a dress or an outfit for me, something special and gorgeous, and he loves when I try it on and I come out of the dressing room (and yes, some dresses look much better on a hanger), and I show him how I look, how the dress looks.

If I buy something without him, he goes a little crazy, just a teeny bit crazy. So, I make sure that Joey goes with me, and that he loves the dresses I try on. I like feeling beautiful for him and I like knowing that he thinks I look beautiful.

The other thing that Joey does for me that I really love, and he does it for me because I never do it for myself, he makes sure that I get a mani-pedi. Yes, fingernails and toe-nails polished.

So, on those special date nights, Joey makes sure I'm taken care of and I have to say that it makes me feel so gorgeous.

REV'S TAKEAWAYS

- Love unconditionally. Not everything is about you. Marriage is not so much gazing into each other's eyes but more looking in the same direction, being on the same page.

- Listen to what your partner is saying. They want you to step back? Step back! But bring by a coffee, or slide a sweet note under the door—show them you're supporting them in other ways. Even if they don't need your help right now, they'll appreciate your love.

- Let your partner solve their own problems; it gives them self-confidence, a good boost, and it feeds their self-esteem. Remember, giving a constant nudge is more about your needs than theirs.

- And last, when they do ask for help, when they do reach out for a hand or a shoulder, never say I told you so. That will just squash all the goodness out of the day.

JUSTINE'S TAKEAWAYS

- Wearing perfume and sexy underwear, and some good old-fashioned flirting, make for a great date night.

- Pick a restaurant you both love, that makes you feel comfortable.

- If your spouse or partner wants to get you a little extra something, like a mani-pedi or a massage, say yes and indulge in the luxury of it.

EPILOGUE

Rev

(OUR HOUSE)

THERE ARE SO MANY THINGS that you need when you're building a house from scratch, from the bottom up.

The list is long, and God is in the details.

Building a house that will last a lifetime or two, a house that can withstand a storm or two or three, is the same as building a good, strong, solid, love-filled marriage.

The thing that I notice a lot is that people want to hurry up and get married, people want to hurry up and build a house, people want to hurry up and have kids and then they want to hurry up and add some more rooms on to the house . . .

Slow down, that's what I want to tell people. Slow down.

It all goes by fast.

One minute you're the hot new rap group and the world is your stage, and the next minute you're at a stage in your life where God is all you need. He is the one watching you. He is your audience. No need to be in a hurry. No need to rush down the aisle, no need to put up a house in two months . . . no need to rush through life.

It takes time to find the right piece of land, to find the right view you want to look out on; it takes time to find the right person to create a life with, to build a life with, to look at life with.

It takes time.

Building a house from scratch, building a marriage from a first date, building a life from the very first step, you have to dig deep so that the foundation that you are building on can last a lifetime. And then, you have to let things settle, let the concrete dry. Let it cure.

What are you building on? Is it love?

Is it protective love, tough love, magical love, trusting love, successful love, good love, enduring love, faithful love, unconditional love, generous love, messy love, grown-up love, attentive love, powerful love, romantic love . . . is it Old School Love?

I was fourteen and I knew that house on the hill with the boxwoods and the flowers that bloomed every Mother's Day would last a lifetime because it was built on love.

I knew that even as a kid.

I knew even if I didn't see it for a while, the house would still be standing.

It would still be beautiful. It would still take my breath away.

You know when something is built on love. It is cared for. It is treated with affection and respect. It is looked at with awe. It is cherished and admired and it isn't taken for granted, not one bit. It is tended to—the roof repaired and the walls repainted and the stone repointed—and its value only appreciates with time.

And you will have a list of all the things you'll be checking off while you're building your house because you don't want to find out a few years later that you let something slip by in the very beginning, something that got your attention but you let it go unattended because you didn't want to deal with it in that moment. You don't want that small unattended thing to turn into something irreparable.

So, no, you can't just put up some walls and put down a floor and think you're ready, set, go.

There is a list of things you need to check off so that you know you are ready to move in. The same holds true with a marriage.

There's a list.

FIRST ON THAT LIST IS love.

Do you love her? Do you love him? Do you love that person enough to set aside some extra love for the days and the nights that are hard, that are filled with pain and unexpected sorrow? Will you have some extra love tucked away somewhere on the days or nights or weeks when you're going to need that extra love because life is weighing you down? Do you have some extra love stashed away on those "just because" days because, yes, extra love is good.

You have to check that off the list.

Love? *Check.*

Then, you have to like the person.

Do you like her? Do you like him? Do they make you laugh? Do they make you smile when you think of them? Do you talk things out and talk things through? Do you share the deep stuff and the light stuff and the everything-in-between stuff? Do you like to do nothing with that person . . . because there is nothing better than that? Do you like to cuddle with each other and giggle and know that's enough to be intimate?

You have to check that off the list.

Like? *Check.*

Are you best friends?

Is she your best friend? Is he your best friend? Because, this here: Being in a marriage with your best friend is the epoxy, the cement, that holds a relationship together. Having a friendship, a good strong solid friendship, goes hand in hand with those sexy romantic sizzling moonlit nights.

You have to check that off the list.

Best friends? *Check.*

Do you still find her sexy and beautiful after all these

years? Do you still find him sexy and beautiful after all these years? Desiring that person, wanting that person, admiring that person, dancing together to the song that only the two of you can hear because it was meant for just the two of you looking at each other from across the room after fifteen, twenty, twenty-five, forty years: Can you still feel your heart beating, racing, pumping?

When you kiss that person, does it taste like magic?

Do you still get butterflies in the pit of your belly?

Sexy? *Check.*

Beautiful? *Check.*

Magic? *Check.*

JUSTINE AND I HAVE BUILT an extraordinary life together, a love-house together—and we started with God as our foundation. We dug deep and we built up. We make sure that things are right with us, that we communicate about everything—the small stuff, the big stuff, the stuff that no one else can see or hear. We repair what is ragged and fraying a bit; we seal up the tiny holes so they don't become big gaping holes. We learned a long time ago that one coat of paint may not be enough and that putting in extra time, one extra coat, makes a huge difference.

We tend to our marriage. We replenish and we refill what might begin to feel a bit depleted, in need of refreshing; we add color and shine if there's any bit of dullness. We both make sure, on a daily basis, that whatever storms come our way, small or big, that we will hold each other up, hold each other tight, until the storm passes through. We make sure our home is still standing.

Our house, our marriage, was built firmly and solidly on love.

Our deep love for God, our deep love for each other, our deep love for our children, our deep love for our family, our deep love for our friends, our deep love for our neighbors, our deep love for love itself—Old School Love.

A little love note for my wife:

MY LOVE ... WHAT I FEEL WHEN WE TALK, WHEN WE COLLABORATE, WHEN WE HAVE OUR MEETINGS ABOUT WHAT WE DO TOGETHER ... IT'S ACTUALLY LIKE THE DAYS RIGHT BEFORE OUR WEDDING ... I GET SHY AND NERVOUS AND EXCITED BECAUSE MY RESPECT FOR YOU IS SO BIG. I HONOR YOU, JUSTINE SIMMONS. WHAT A GEM YOU ARE. I LOVE YOU!! MY PROMISE TO YOU IS CONTINUED ROMANCE, LOVE, RESPECT, AND PLEASING SURPRISES JUST LIKE THE DAY WE MET. MY ENERGY OF HOPING TO KEEP THOSE BUTTERFLIES IN YOUR STOMACH REMAINS. FOREVER MY VALENTINE.

AFTERWORD

Justine's Mom

SUSAN PATRICIA YOUNG,
JULY 31, 1942–APRIL 22, 2019

Although she was battling cancer, Justine Simmons's mom unexpectedly died from pneumonia on April 22, 2019.

Rev

(A TRIBUTE TO MY MOTHER-IN-LAW)

SHE LOVED ME. I always knew she loved me by the way she treated me like a son, her son.

In my memory, she was always kind and generous toward me, and it made me want to reciprocate the kindness and generosity.

I would spoil her by taking her to fancy dinners, or spa treatments, or by flying her out to Vegas when I was performing there. She loved being included, but she wasn't caught up in my celebrity. She liked my character, she knew I was a nice person, and she loved the way I treated her and our family—and most important of all, how I treat Justine.

Her loving me made me know that I was doing right by Justine. And if I weren't, trust me, she would have said something. She wasn't one to hold back or keep her mouth shut. She was as truthful as the day is long.

Our kids loved her. "Grandma's coming," they would say with such enthusiasm before a visit. She came to our house for holidays, Thanksgiving and Christmas, and she was on our show, *Rev Run's Sunday Suppers*. She loved our show's holiday special episodes.

She always came through for us, for the kids. We could call her on a moment's notice and she would be here in a flash, no questions asked. She was reliable and dependable. I couldn't have gotten through Diggy's birth, or Justine's hospitalization, without her.

More than anything, she was the most courageous woman I knew, beyond courageous. And she was tougher than anybody, but not mean tough, not cruel tough, not nasty tough; she was bold tough and brave tough and quietly strong tough.

She beat cancer three times.

When I asked her once about the cancer, because it had returned, she said, "Don't worry, Joey, I kicked its butt before, and I'll kick it again."

In her mind, she was going to destroy cancer; she was going to come through with flying colors. In her mind, it was like having a cold or the flu, and she just had to show cancer who was the boss. She never let it keep her down for long, even when the cancer returned and she had another bout of chemo. She treated it like an unwanted visitor. *Can't stay here . . . you gotta go on your way* is how she viewed cancer and all the treatments.

During the last months of her life, we did everything

we could to make her feel special. Every single weekend I would pick her up on Long Island, where she lived, and take her to her favorite restaurants—she loved crab legs—and all her favorite places until she could no longer do any of that.

She was an extraordinary woman, and she will undoubtedly live on in our hearts and in our lives and in our children.

Justine

(REST IN PEACE AND REST IN POWER)

MY MOM WAS ALWAYS SO PROUD OF ME, always encouraging and confident.

Her confidence in me was so contagious that it, in turn, filled me with confidence.

I think there was a time when I was younger, though, when I couldn't *see* that confidence. She was a strong and silent woman, and I thought that since she didn't seem overly concerned about me, maybe she just didn't care so much.

She didn't seem to worry about me when I would go out as a teenager. She never made me call her, like most of my friends' parents made them do, to say when I was coming home or where I was. She would never hound me, never check up on me.

I was independent and strong, too. I started working when I was fifteen years old. I bought my own car, and I got my own apartment, and I never asked her to help me. I was always so self-sufficient and so determined; her strength, the power of her character, rubbed off on me.

Right before she passed away, I asked her about that; I asked why she didn't hound me when I was out and about when I was younger, and she said that she trusted me.

"I trusted you."

It was just that simple.

That was such a huge thing to hear; it wasn't because she wasn't interested, it wasn't because she didn't care—it was because she knew she could trust me, because she had confidence in me, in the choices I was making.

She loved me so very much.

It's so funny because, as a mom, I am the opposite with my kids. I love them, and I worry about them—and believe me, they know it. They have to call, they have to tell me when they're coming home, they have to tell me where they are . . . and it's because I get so nervous.

But hearing my mom tell me that she trusted me . . . well, that made me think about how I can be less nervous with my kids, more trusting. That is something I really want to work on, something to do in her memory for my kids.

My mom was such an amazing mentor to me; she led by example, and she taught me through her actions: the way she handled adversity and pain, the way she handled her cancer and cancer treatments and the recurrence of that disease. Her courage will stay with me, in me, always.

She was such a warm person, such a loving person, and she was deeply loved in return. People just loved her.

And boy, was she honest about her feelings. If she didn't like something, she would tell you. She wasn't afraid to speak her truth, because she knew that if she loved you and you loved her back she could tell you anything. She really believed that loving someone wasn't just sharing the nice, good stuff; she believed that love was about sharing your feelings, the good and the bad, and she also made it easy to be able to tell her anything.

We used to speak, if not every day, at least every other day, and I will miss those conversations so very much. I will miss her voice. I will miss her terribly.

I'm so glad she was my mom.

ACKNOWLEDGMENTS

WE MUST START BY THANKING God for bestowing all of his beautiful gifts upon us during our lifetime.

Thanks to our parents for molding us into who we are today. We learned about life, love, and respect from you.

To our children, Vanessa, Angela, JoJo, Diggy, Russy, and Miley. We love you and adore you each and every day.

We need to thank Amy Ferris for her enthusiasm about this book, and Ken Ferris for his joyful support.

We also wish to thank the entire team at HarperCollins, especially Lisa Sharkey and Anna Montague for helping guide this to fruition.

Finally, we must thank our manager, Michael Lehman, for always being there for us and for making us feel that we can accomplish all things.

ABOUT THE AUTHORS

JOSEPH "REV RUN" SIMMONS, the front man of the seminal hip-hop group RUN DMC, has sold tens of millions of records around the world and is widely credited for ushering rap music into mainstream culture. Recently inducted into the Rock & Roll Hall of Fame, the group was also the first rap act to earn a Grammy Lifetime Achievement Award. Rev Run remains a dynamic figure in entertainment today, and along with his wife of more than twenty-five years, Justine, has starred on shows including *Run's House*, *All About the Washingtons*, and *Rev Run's Sunday Suppers*. Through their television endeavors, and their book *Take Back Your Family: A Challenge to America's Parents*, Rev Run and Justine strive to make their family values, humor, and spirituality as visible as possible. Family remains their biggest focus, and their playful, loving relationship is an inspiration to many.